ADDICTION AND GRACE

ADDICTION
AND GRACE

Gerald G. May, M.D.

HarperSanFrancisco
A Division of HarperCollinsPublishers

For Ray,

With affection and gratitude

FIRST HARPERCOLLINS PAPERBACK EDITION PUBLISHED IN 1991.

Library of Congress Cataloging-in-Publication Data

May, Gerald G.
    Addiction and grace / Gerald G. May.
        p.   cm.
    Includes index.
    ISBN 0-06-065537-2
    1. Compulsive behavior—Religious aspects—Christianity.
    2. Substance abuse—Religious aspects—Christianity.   I. Title.
    [RC533.M39   1991]
    616.86—dc20   90–43077
                                                                        CIP

91   92   93   94   95   M-V   10   9   8   7   6   5   4   3   2

Contents

Preface

The writing of this book has been a true journey for me, filled not only with the usual ups and downs of authoring, but also with prayer and real spiritual warfare. It has been, in a way, the kind of spiritual desert and garden I will be describing toward the end of the book. Many of the old understandings to which I had been addicted were stripped away, leaving a desertlike spaciousness where my customary props and securities no longer existed. Grace was able to flow into this emptiness, and something new was able to grow. Fresh understandings took root, and the insights that emerged were clearer, simpler, and more beautiful. I became acutely aware of living what I was writing about. I live a life infused by the bondage of addiction and the hope of grace; I think we all live such lives. My hope is that you who read these words will be touched lovingly by the True Word, that there will be enough space within my words for grace to flow for you.

In reading this text, you should keep in mind that although I consider myself a reasonably careful scientist, I am neither a trained theologian nor a scriptural scholar. This book is full of my own theological assumptions which, although honestly and accurately reflecting my experience, are only partially systematized or externally justified. I ask you, then, not to read my words as authority, but to let them resonate where and how they will, with your own experience and sense of truth.

I have taken considerable liberties in my use of Scripture. I felt this was permissible because my use of Scripture in this book is solely for elucidating basic themes, not for authority or justification. In bringing the quotations together, I have relied on a wide variety of translations, and in a number of places I have combined several translations within the same quotation.

And, as with the prologue to John's Gospel quoted at the beginning of chapter 6, I have even taken a stab at my own translations. This process has been a rich and deep encounter with Scripture for me, and I hope it will also bring some fresh insights to you. Bear in mind, however, that my versions are not necessarily authoritative; I encourage you to read the references for yourself in your own most trusted translation(s).

The primary scriptural themes for this text are the Eden story (Genesis 1:27–3:24), the exodus experience (Exodus 1–15), and Paul's beautiful portrayal of sin, deliverance, and the life of the Spirit in the Letter to the Romans (5:12–8:39). I encourage you to read these sections of the Bible before beginning the main text of this book and to refer to them periodically as you proceed. Doing this will, I am sure, add much to the value of the book for you.

In the service of confidentiality, vignettes concerning people in this text are composites based on real people's experience. They do not refer to specific individuals. Footnotes are scattered like freckles throughout the text. Insofar as possible, do not let them interfere with your reading. They either simply give references or elaborate on points made within the text; they can be reviewed at a later time or not at all. Wherever I could, I have placed them at the ends of paragraphs to make them a bit less intrusive.

I have long considered it a creative challenge to use inclusive language in writing, and I have tried to be especially careful in this book. This effort may not keep me or my ideas from being sexist, but it does help my use of words. In this regard, I have not only avoided gender-specific words in my own writing, but also have edited a number of quotations from other writings. Where I have done this, I am convinced that the author's meaning has been enhanced rather than impaired, but references are cited for all major quotations so that readers can judge for themselves.

My deepest human indebtedness in this work is to those chemically addicted people and their families who have allowed me to share some of their experience. They taught me that major addiction is the sacred disease of our time. In addition, innumerable other individuals have contributed in ways great and small to this endeavor. This book comes as part of an exploration of spirituality and the human brain that I am conducting under the auspices of the Shalem Institute for Spiritual Formation, Mount Saint Alban, Washington, D.C. 20016. I am grateful to the administration and staff of Shalem for their hearty and prayerful support of this work, and to the many friends of Shalem who have given of their resources and time to make it possible. It is wonderful that there are so many of you that I cannot mention you by name. Let us pray that our communal efforts will contribute to that primal, eternal desire that we all share with God: perfect freedom and love for all humankind.

1. DESIRE: Addiction and Human Freedom

Where your treasure is, there will your heart be also.

THE GOSPEL ACCORDING TO MATTHEW

After twenty years of listening to the yearnings of people's hearts, I am convinced that all human beings have an inborn desire for God. Whether we are consciously religious or not, this desire is our deepest longing and our most precious treasure. It gives us meaning. Some of us have repressed this desire, burying it beneath so many other interests that we are completely unaware of it. Or we may experience it in different ways—as a longing for wholeness, completion, or fulfillment. Regardless of how we describe it, it is a longing for love. It is a hunger to love, to be loved, and to move closer to the Source of love. This yearning is the essence of the human spirit; it is the origin of our highest hopes and most noble dreams.

Modern theology describes this desire as God given. In an outpouring of love, God creates us and plants the seeds of this desire within us. Then, throughout our lives, God nourishes this desire, drawing us toward fulfillment of the two great commandments: "Thou shalt love thy God with all thy heart, and thy neighbor as thyself." If we could claim our longing for love as the true treasure of our hearts, we would, with God's grace, be able to live these commandments.[1]

But something gets in the way. Not only are we unable to fulfill the commandments; we often even ignore our desire to do so. The longing at the center of our hearts repeatedly disappears from our awareness, and its energy is usurped by forces that are not at all loving. Our desires are captured, and we give ourselves over to things that, in our deepest honesty, we really do not want. There are times when each of us can easily identify with the words of the apostle Paul: "I do not understand my own behavior; I do not act as I mean to, but I do the things that I hate. Though the will to do what is good is in me, the power to do it is not; the good thing I want to do, I never do; the evil thing which I do not want—that is what I do."[2]

In writing these words, Paul was talking about sin. Theologically, sin is what turns us away from love—away from love for ourselves, away from love for one another, and away from love for God. When I look at this problem psychologically, I see two forces that are responsible: repression and addiction. We all suffer from both repression and addiction. Of the two, repression is by far the milder one.

Repression

We frequently repress our desire for love because love makes us vulnerable to being hurt. The word *passion*, which is used to express strong loving desire, comes from the Latin root *passus*, which means "suffered." All of us know that, along with bringing joy, love can make us suffer. Often we repress our desire for love to minimize this suffering. This happens after someone spurns our love; we stifle our desire, and it may take us a long time before we are ready to love again. It is a normal human response; we repress our longings when they hurt us too much. Perhaps it is not surprising, then, that we do the same with our deepest longings for God. God does not always come to us in the pleasant ways we might expect, and so we repress our desire for God.

When we repress a desire, we try to keep it out of our awareness. We try to keep our focus on other things—safer things. Psychology calls this *displacement*. But something that has been repressed does not really go away; it remains within us, skirting the edges of our consciousness. Every now and then it reminds us of its presence, as if to say, "Remember me?" And, when we are ready to tackle the thing again, we can. We may repress our longing for God, but, like the hound of heaven that it is, it haunts us. And it is there for us to deal with whenever we are ready. Repression, then, in spite of its sinister reputation, is relatively flexible. It is workable. Addiction, the other force that turns us away from love, is much more vicious.

The Paradoxes of Addiction

For generations, psychologists thought that virtually all self-defeating behavior was caused by repression. I have now come to believe that addiction is a separate and even more self-defeating force that abuses our freedom and makes us do things we really do not want to do. While repression stifles desire, addiction *attaches* desire, bonds and enslaves the energy of desire to certain specific behaviors, things, or people. These objects of attachment then become preoccupations and obsessions; they come to rule our lives.

The word *attachment* has long been used by spiritual traditions to describe this process. It comes from the old French *a-tache*, meaning "nailed to." Attachment "nails" our desire to specific objects and creates addiction. In this light, we can see why traditional psychotherapy, which is based on the release of repression, has proven ineffective with addictions. It also shows why addiction is the most powerful psychic enemy of humanity's desire for God.

I am not being flippant when I say that all of us suffer from addiction. Nor am I reducing the meaning of addiction. I mean in all truth that the psychological, neurological, and spiritual dynamics of full-fledged addiction are actively at work within every human being. The same processes that are responsible for addiction to alcohol and narcotics are also responsible for addiction to ideas, work, relationships, power, moods, fantasies, and an endless variety of other things. We are all addicts in every sense of the word. Moreover, our addictions are our own worst enemies. They enslave us with chains that are of our own making and yet that, paradoxically, are virtually beyond our control. Addiction also makes idolators of us all, because it forces us to worship these objects of attachment, thereby preventing us from truly, freely loving God and one another. Addiction breeds willfulness within us, yet, again paradoxically, it erodes our free will and eats away at our dignity. Addiction, then, is at once an inherent part of our nature and an antagonist of our nature. It is the absolute enemy of human freedom, the antipathy of love. Yet, in still another paradox, our addictions can lead us to a deep appreciation of grace. They can bring us to our knees.

The paradoxes of addiction raise many questions. What really is addiction? What is its spiritual significance, its true relationship to grace? What is the difference between addiction and deeply, passionately caring about something or someone? Are there some good addictions? And if traditional psychology does not help addiction, what does? I think I can shed some light on these questions, but many of the answers will not be pleasant to hear. Addiction is not something we can simply take care of by applying the proper remedy, for it is in the very nature of addiction to feed on our attempts to master it.

At the outset, I must confess that I have by no means achieved victory over my own addictions. I am riddled with them, and I further confess that I enjoy some of them immensely. Although deep in my heart I would prefer to be free of them, the larger part of myself simply does not want to give them up. It is characteristic for addiction to mix one's motives. But although I often feel impotent before my addictions, I do have some understanding of them, and that is what I hope to share with you. Understanding will not deliver us from addiction, but it will, I hope, help us appreciate grace. Grace is the most powerful force in the universe. It can transcend repression, addiction, and every other internal or external power that seeks to oppress the freedom of the human heart. Grace is where our hope lies.

Journey Toward Understanding

It was in working with some of the most tragically addicted people—those enslaved to narcotics and alcohol—that I began wondering about addiction and grace. It was there also that I began to recognize my own addictedness. Most importantly, it was in the course of that work that I reclaimed my own spiritual hunger, a desire for God and for love that for many years I had tried to repress.

As nearly as I can recall, the repression of my spiritual desire began shortly after my father died. I was nine at the time. Prior to that, I had had a comfortable relationship with God. As with all children, the earliest years of my life were "simply religious." In the innocent wonder and awe of early childhood awareness, everything just *is* spiritual. My religious education had given me a name for God, but I hardly needed it. I prayed easily; God was a friend.[3]

In a reaction typical for a nine year old, I expected God to somehow keep me in touch with my father after his death. I prayed for this, but of course it did not happen. As a result, something hurt and angry in me, something deeper than my consciousness, chose to dispense with God. I would take care of myself; I would go it alone. My wanting—my love—had caused me to be hurt, and something in me decided not to want so much. I repressed my longing. Just as my father faded from my awareness, so did God, and so did my desire for God.

During college, I fell in love with literature and philosophy. In retrospect, I think this was my desire for God surfacing again, as a search for beauty and truth. I even tried to go to church on occasion, but I wasn't consciously looking for God. By then I was searching for something that I could use to develop a sense of mastery over my life, something that would help me go it alone. In medical school and psychiatric training,

I tried to make a god out of science; science seemed learnable, masterable, and controllable. Throughout, I resisted prayer and rebelled at religiosity in others. Such things seemed immature; they were signs of weakness. I wanted to be autonomous, although I wasn't completely sure what the word meant.

I was in the Air Force during the Vietnam War. Much in the Vietnam experience I had to repress. But much of it I could not repress. In a way, the tragedy of Vietnam woke me up a little. Afterward, I took a position as director of a community drug abuse clinic. With all the energy that might be expected of a young doctor, I applied my best psychiatric methods to the treatment of addictions. None of them worked. I was able to help people with their emotional and social problems, but they remained addicted to chemicals. Since so much of my desire for meaning and wholeness had become attached to professional success, and I was not being successful, I started to become depressed. A colleague called it a "normal professional depression." He went on to say, "All decent psychiatrists experience such depressions when they can't cure the people they treat. If you didn't feel depressed, it would mean you didn't care enough." It was some consolation. But not much.

Then one day in the middle of this depression, I was casually introduced to a faith healer at a conference in a nearby town. I did not believe in faith healers. As we shook hands, she paused, holding my hand, and told me she thought I was meant to be a healer too, but "I wouldn't take my dog to you, because you think you are the one that has to do the healing." These are not the words one might expect to be helpful for a depressed person. But they struck me deep and well. In my search for self-determination, I had also been trying to command the very process of healing. It was obvious that some change in attitude was called for. I still wasn't certain, however, what form that change should take.

At about the same time, I embarked on a little informal research. I identified a few people who seemed to have overcome serious addictions to alcohol and other drugs, and I asked them what had helped them turn their lives around so dramatically. All of them described some sort of spiritual experience. They kindly acknowledged their appreciation for the professional help they had received, but they also made it clear that this help had not been the source of their healing. What had healed them was something spiritual. They didn't all use religious terms, but there was no doubt in my mind that what they spoke of was spiritual. Something about what they said reminded me of home. It had something to do with turning to God.

As a result, I relaxed a little. I honestly considered there might be some power greater than myself involved in healing, and that I might be better off cooperating with that power instead of trying to usurp it. I also set about trying to understand more of what constituted "spiritual experience," and why it had been so helpful to these addicted people. Secretly, I wanted to learn how to "do it" to people as part of their therapy. Even more secretly, I wanted to have those kinds of experiences once again myself.

I described these spiritual experiences to some clergy friends. Most of them didn't seem to understand what I was talking about. The least helpful friends tried to give me Freudian explanations of oceanic experiences: "Why, it's simply a narcissistic regression of the ego to a state of infantile dissociation in order to avoid reality issues that have stimulated unacceptable libidinous impulses." They said such things as if I should have known them already. But that was the problem; I did know them already, and knowing them didn't help. But two of my clergy colleagues did offer some help. They said, in effect, "We don't know for sure what it is either, but we agree it's spiritual, and we'd like to help you explore it." Interestingly, these two knew more psychological theory than the others; they knew enough to realize that psychology was not going to answer everything.

With their companionship, I explored a multitude of spiritual ways and means. The 1960s were turning into the 1970s, and Freud and white-knuckled social activism were beginning to give way to something fresh afoot in America, something a little more spiritual. I studied Eastern religions, psychic phenomena, psychedelic drugs, biofeedback, all the great stew of psycho-spiritual pop and pap that was percolating across the nation at the time. I read Alan Watts and Baba Ram Dass. I meditated every day. From a comfortable distance, I watched the rise of the charismatic renewal in Christian churches, and, from an equal distance, I sensed something powerful I couldn't understand in Alcoholics Anonymous.

One evening, about six months after my quest began, I was diligently practicing a form of yoga meditation that encourages the free coming and going of all thoughts. It is a method that might be described as the opposite of repression. In the freedom I gave to my mind, one of the thoughts that came was prayer. It was, in the beginning, the prayer of a nine year old, embarrassingly immature. "Dear Jesus, help me." I would have stifled it immediately had I not been dutifully allowing all my thoughts to come and go. It was a sad and painful thing just to let that prayer happen, but I did. As months and years passed, the prayer grew, and with it, my awareness of my desire for God.

I realized my exploration was less a professional research project and more a personal spiritual journey. I was not in control of my life; I needed as much of God's grace as any of my patients did. With that growing realization, my spiritual desire seemed to pick up where it had left off some twenty years earlier. Now it was out in the light again, and I gradually became able to reclaim it as my true heart's desire and the most precious thing in my life.

My more scientific observations continued, and for the most part they seemed to nourish and be nourished by the spiritual desire within me. The first, most striking, observation was that people could become addicted to chemicals that weren't supposed to be addictive. In those days (and even until recently) drugs such as LSD, marijuana, and cocaine were not considered addictive. According to the experts, one might develop psychological dependency and overdo these drugs, but the drugs themselves were not supposed to be physically addictive. Evidence for physical addiction required withdrawal symptoms and tolerance (the need for increasing amounts). Yet in my clinical practice I saw many people who in fact did have such symptoms with these drugs, and with a host of other substances as well. Someone walked in who was addicted to propoxyphene, a common painkiller that was supposed to be no more addictive than aspirin. Then someone came in addicted to aspirin! Then nose drops. Antidepressants. Tranquilizers. The patients showed true addictions, complete with withdrawal symptoms and tolerance. It occurred to me that if a substance could alter your mind in any way whatsoever, it was possible to become addicted to it.

I realized that I myself was addicted to a variety of substances: nicotine, caffeine, sugar, and chocolate, to name a few. Was this "physical addiction" or just "psychological dependency"? Surely my tolerance and withdrawal symptoms were not as severe as I had observed in people addicted to alcohol or pure heroin, but the differences seemed only in degree. If I didn't pay attention to my intake of these substances, I would increase my use of them. I would want more. That is a mild form of tolerance. And if I tried to cut down or quit completely I would experience distress, a distress that was in no way as dramatic as that of my patients, but neither was it just in my mind. The distress was a kind of tension; my muscles would be tighter than normal and a little tremulous, and there might be a headache and irritability, or even a slightly queasy stomach. From a physiologic standpoint, I was experiencing mild reflections of the same symptoms my patients experienced in withdrawal from narcotics.

Finally, I realized that for both myself and other people, addictions are not limited to substances. I was also addicted to work, performance, responsibility, intimacy, being liked, helping others, and an almost endless list of other behaviors. At the time, it seemed just fine to be addicted to some of these things, but others I would have much preferred to be free of. I had to admit that I had not freely chosen these things; my concern for them was not something I could control. They were compulsions.

Tolerance and withdrawal were definite. However much achievement, intimacy, or approval I had, it was never quite enough. I always wanted more. And if I had to do without one of them, I would experience not only a craving for it, but also some degree of anxiety and even actual physical discomfort. It occurred to me that my original "professional depression" had happened because I had been addicted to success and control. It was, in fact, a withdrawal; it happened when I couldn't get my fix of professional success.

Even my littlest bad habits and secret fantasies had the qualities of addiction. I tried to take comfort in saying, "Yes, but my bad habits are inconsequential compared to alcoholism or drug addiction." That statement was certainly true, but it also felt like a self-justification, a rationalization for keeping my habits going. It sounded too much like alcoholics I had heard saying, "Well, at least we're not junkies," while on the other side of the same hospital ward narcotic addicts were saying, "Well, at least we're not winos."

I can honestly say, then, that it was my my work with addicted people, and the consequent realization of my own addictive behavior, that brought me to my knees. I am glad. Grace was there. If my attachments had not caused me to fail miserably at controlling my life and work, I doubt I ever would have recovered the spiritual desire and the sense of God that had been so precious to me as a child. Compared to what happens to people who suffer from alcoholism or narcotic addiction, what happened to me may not seem much of a "rock bottom." But it had the same grace-full effect. To state it quite simply, I had tried to run my life on the basis of my own willpower alone. When my supply of success at this egotistic autonomy ran out, I became depressed. And with the depression, by means of grace, came a chance for spiritual openness.

I never did learn how to make spiritual experiences happen to chemically addicted people so their lives would be transformed. I didn't learn much of anything that helped me treat addictions, or for that matter any other form of illness. But I did become slightly more humble, through a growing appreciation of what I could and could not do to help myself or anyone else. I also learned that all people are addicts, and that addictions to alcohol and other drugs are simply more obvious and tragic addictions than others have. To be alive is to be addicted, and to be alive and addicted is to stand in need of grace.

Genesis

The journey I have just described eventually led me to full-time work in exploring the interfaces of psychology and spirituality. I wrote five books on the subject. This is the sixth. A few years ago, I was given the opportunity to review current neurological research to see how it might inform our appreciation of spiritual growth. In this exploration I discovered that neurology was on the brink of understanding how addiction takes place in the brain. To me, these neurological insights harmonized beautifully with what spiritual authorities have been saying for thousands of years. This book is the integration of these themes. The themes themselves began long ago, with the biblical story of creation.

The book of Genesis says that God made Adam and Eve out of earth and breath on the sixth day of creation and gave them an earthly paradise, a garden, to live in. It is said that this garden was near a place called Eden, which means "delight." God looked on these two human beings and saw that they were very good and blessed them. God told Eve and Adam that they could eat fruit from all the trees in the garden except for two: the tree of immortality and the tree of the knowledge of good and evil. But a snake told Eve that God was lying, that she could indeed eat the fruit from the tree of knowledge, and that she would become like a god if she did. Seeing how enticing the forbidden fruit looked, she tried some. Then she gave some to Adam as well. When God confronted the two human beings with what they had done, Adam blamed Eve. And Eve blamed the snake.

Adam and Eve's behavior is usually interpreted as symbolizing humanity's ongoing willful rebelliousness against God. God creates us with free will, and we respond by trying to be gods. We want to be the masters of our own destiny. We keep trying to substitute our own will for God's will, but our pride always brings us to a fall and thrusts us even further away from an Eden we had hoped to recapture on our own terms. I certainly think this portrayal of human willfulness is accurate.[4]

But when I read the Genesis story carefully, I respond sympathetically toward Eve and Adam. Surely they are responsible for what they do, but they do not really seem like hostile rebels; instead they seem innocent and gullible, almost like little children. As the Scripture relates it, they ate the fruit not because it was forbidden, but because it was "enticing to look at and good to eat" and because the serpent told them they could become like gods if they ate it. It seems to me their real problem was not rebelliousness but foolishness. Their lack of wisdom made them exceedingly vulnerable to temptation. Once they gave in to that temptation, their freedom was invaded by attachment. They experienced the need for more. God knew that then they would not—*could not*—stop with just the one tree. "They must not be allowed to stretch out their hands and pick from the tree of life also." So God made a set of clothes for each of them and sent them out of the garden.[5]

In this powerful story, the basic elements of addiction and grace are distilled: freedom, willfulness, desire, temptation, attachment, and, of course, the fall. It seems to me that each of our addictions reenacts Eve and Adam's story. The story of Eden is not over, yet neither is it simply repeating itself endlessly through history. Instead, it is going somewhere. I believe that humankind's ongoing struggle with addiction is preparing the ground of perfect love.

Addiction and Freedom

God creates us out of love, or perhaps, as the fourteenth-century German mystic Meister Eckhart is supposed to have said, out of the laughter of the Trinity, which is the same thing.[6] Scripture proclaims that this love, from which and for which we are created, is perfect. I do not presume to fully understand what this perfect love means, but I am certain that it draws us toward itself by means of our own deepest desires. I am also certain that this love wants us to have free will. We are intended to make free choices. Psychologically, we are not completely determined by our conditioning; we are not puppets or automatons. Spiritually, our freedom allows us to choose as we wish for or against God, life, and love. The love that creates us may be haunting, but it is not enslaving; it is eternally present, yet endlessly open.[7]

It seems to me that free will is given to us for a purpose: so that we may choose freely, without coercion or manipulation, to love God in return, and to love one another in a similarly perfect way. This is the deepest desire of our hearts. In other words, our creation is by love, in love, and for love. It is both our birthright and our authentic destiny to participate fully in this creative loving, and freedom of will is essential for our participation to occur.[8]

But our freedom is not complete. Working against it is the powerful force of addiction. Psychologically, addiction *uses up* desire. It is like a psychic malignancy, sucking our life energy into specific obsessions and compulsions, leaving less and less energy available for other people and other pursuits. Spiritually, addiction is a deep-seated form of idolatry. The objects of our addictions become our false gods. These are what we worship, what we attend to, where we give our time and energy, *instead of love*. Addiction, then, displaces and supplants God's love as the source and object of our deepest true desire. It is, as one modern spiritual writer has called it, a "counterfeit of religious presence."[9]

Attachment and Detachment

Addiction exists wherever persons are internally compelled to give energy to things that are not their true desires. To define it directly, addiction is a *state* of compulsion, obsession, or preoccupation that enslaves a person's will and desire. Addiction sidetracks and eclipses the energy of our deepest, truest desire for love and goodness. We succumb because the energy of our desire becomes attached, nailed, to specific behaviors, objects, or people. *Attachment*, then, is the process that enslaves desire and creates the state of addiction.

The great spiritual traditions of the world have been talking about attachment for millennia. The Upanishads of ancient India go back as early as ten centuries before Christ. One of these says, "When all desires that cling to the heart are surrendered, then a mortal becomes immortal." In the sixth century B.C., the Greek Heraclitus said of attachment, "Whatever it wishes to get, it purchases at the cost of soul." In the Hebrew tradition, the ancient preacher of Ecclesiastes moaned, "I denied my eyes nothing that they desired, refused my heart no pleasure. . . . What futility it all was, what chasing after the wind." The core tenets of Buddhism are the Four Noble Truths: (1) suffering is a fact of life; (2) suffering is caused by attachment; (3) liberation from suffering and the reinstitution of human freedom can happen only through *det*achment; and (4) human effort toward detachment must involve all aspects of one's life in a deeply spiritual way.[10]

Detachment is the word used in spiritual traditions to describe freedom of desire. Not freedom *from* desire, but freedom *of* desire. Of all the concepts we will be discussing, detachment is the most widely misunderstood. For centuries, people have distorted its meaning, mistakenly assuming that detachment devalues desire and denies the potential goodness of the things and people to which one can become attached. Thus detachment has come to be associated with coldness, austerity, and lack of passion. This is simply not true. An authentic spiritual understanding of detachment devalues neither desire nor the objects of desire. Instead, it "aims at correcting one's own anxious grasping in order to free oneself for committed relationship to God."[11] According to Meister Eckhart, detachment "enkindles the heart, awakens the spirit, stimulates our longings, and shows us where God is. . . ."[12]

Detachment uncovers our basic desire for God and sets it free. With freedom of desire comes the capacity to love, and love is the goal of the spiritual life. Jesus' many words about detachment are set in the context of growing fullness of love.[13] In Buddhism's Metta Sutra, we find the following: "Let your senses be controlled . . . and in this way become truly loving. . . . Even as a mother watches over and protects her child . . . so with a boundless mind should one cherish all beings, radiating friendliness over the entire world, above, below, and all around without limit." The theme continues in Taoism: "The sage . . . is detached, thus at one with all. Love the world as your own self; then you can truly care for all things." And it echoes in the Bhagavad Gita, the great Hindu Song of God: "Only by love can people see me, and know me, and come unto me. Those who work for me, who love me, whose End Supreme I am, free from attachment to all things, and with love for all creation, they in truth come to me."[14]

So instead of promoting a dry, uncaring state, detachment does just the opposite. It seeks a liberation of desire, an enhancement of passion, the freedom to love with all one's being, and the willingness to bear the pain such love can bring. In contemporary spiritual circles, some people wish to use the term *nonattachment* instead of *detachment* in order to temper some of these old misconceptions. The term may be useful in some settings. However, here we are speaking of attachment as the process through which desire becomes enslaved and addictions are created. It is most accurate, then, to use *detachment* to describe the opposite process, the liberation of desire. The state that liberation leads to might legitimately be called a condition of nonattachment. I, however, prefer to call it freedom.

Grace

The first and greatest commandment for both Judaism and Christianity is, "You shall have no other gods before me." Similarly, Islam's basic creed begins with "There is no god but God."[15] It is no accident that these three great monotheistic religions share this fundamental assertion. "Nothing," God says, "must be more important to you than I am. I am the Ultimate Value, by whom the value of all other things must be measured and in whom true love for all other things must be found." We have already mentioned the two commandments that Jesus called the greatest: "You shall love the Lord your God with all your heart, with all your soul, and with all your strength, and you shall love your neighbor as yourself." It is addiction that keeps our love for God and neighbor incomplete. It is addiction that creates other gods for us. Because of our addictions, we will always be storing up treasures somewhere other than heaven, and these treasures will kidnap our hearts and souls and strength.

Because of our addictions, we simply cannot—on our own—keep the great commandments. Most of us have tried, again and again, and failed. Some of us have even recognized that these commandments are really our own deepest desires. We have tried to dedicate our lives to them, but still we fail. I think our failure is necessary, for it is in failure and helplessness that we can most honestly and completely turn to grace. Grace is our only hope for dealing with addiction, the only power that can truly vanquish its destructiveness. Grace is the invincible advocate of freedom and the absolute expression of perfect love.

Some Christian spiritual authorities criticize other religions for denying the reality of grace. But in fact grace has its counterparts in all religions. The Torah of Judaism is suffused with cries for God's loving salvation. Islam finds its very heart in Allah's mercy. Even for Buddhists and Hindus, with all their emphasis on personal practice and effort, there could be no liberation without the grace of the Divine. Tibetan Buddhists, for example, pray for "gift waves" from deities and gurus. A

Tibetan Buddhist hymn pleads simply, "Please bestow your compassionate grace upon us." In the Bhagavad Gita, the Hindu God proclaims, "United with me, you shall overcome all difficulties, by my grace. Fear no longer, for I will save you from sin and from bondage." And in the twentieth century, Mohandas Gandhi was very clear: "Without devotion and the consequent grace of God, humanity's endeavor is vain."[16]

I do not wish to imply that all religions are basically the same; they certainly are not. But I do wish to demonstrate that in spite of widely varying emphases and radical differences in theology, all major religions deal centrally with the basic themes I have set forth here: we are created for love and freedom, addiction hinders us, and grace is necessary for salvation.

For Christians, grace is the dynamic outpouring of God's loving nature that flows into and through creation in an endless self-offering of healing, love, illumination, and reconciliation. It is a gift that we are free to ignore, reject, ask for, or simply accept. And it is a gift that is often given in spite of our intentions and errors. At such times, when grace is so clearly given unrequested, uninvited, even undeserved, there can be no authentic response but gratitude and awe.

It is possible to approach grace as if it were just another thing to be addicted to, something we could collect or hoard. But this kind of grasping can capture only an image of grace. Grace itself cannot be possessed; it is eternally free, and like the Spirit that gives it, it blows where it will. We can seek it and try to be open to it, but we cannot control it.[17]

Similarly, grace seeks us but will not control us. Saint Augustine once said that God is always trying to give good things to us, but our hands are too full to receive them. If our hands are full, they are full of the things to which we are addicted. And not only our hands, but also our hearts, minds, and attention are clogged with addiction. Our addictions fill up the spaces within us, spaces where grace might flow.

It is most important to remember, however, that it is not the objects of our addictions that are to blame for filling up our hands and hearts; it is our clinging to these objects, grasping for them, becoming obsessed with them. In the words of John of the Cross, "It is not the things of this world that either occupy the soul or cause it harm, since they enter it not, but rather the will and desire for them." This will and desire, this clinging and grasping, is attachment.[18]

Hope

It appears, then, that we are in a predicament. We are dependent upon grace for liberation from our addictions, but those very addictions impair our receptivity to grace. The message may not sound like good news. Yet God creates and cares for us in such a way that our addictions can never *completely* vanquish our freedom. Addiction may oppress our desire, erode our wills, confound our motivations, and contaminate our judgment, but its bondage is never absolute.

Because of God's continuing love, the human spirit can never be completely obliterated. No matter how oppressed we are, by other people and circumstances or by our own internal addictions, some small capacity for choice remains unvanquished. Poets have written beautifully about this indomitability of the human spirit, but its most eloquent advocates are men and women who have given their lives in the struggle against social oppression. Mohandas Gandhi used the term *soul force* to describe the internal undying ember of freedom, and he centered his doctrine of nonviolence upon it. Martin Luther King spoke of the same thing when he said, "I refuse to accept the idea that the 'is-ness' of our present nature makes us morally incapable of reaching up for the 'ought-ness' that forever confronts us." A young Jewish child of the holocaust must have felt the same thing when he wrote, "And every day, no matter how bitter it be, I will say: From tomorrow on, I shall be sad, Not today!" The bare edge of freedom is insured and preserved inside us by God, and no matter what forces oppress us from without or within, it is indestructible.[19]

Because of our eternal possibility for freedom, it is no more hopeless to be defeated by our own interior addictions than by external oppression. Although we cannot rid ourselves of attachment through our own autonomous efforts, and our addictions can indeed deaden our responsiveness to grace, there is always some level at which we can choose, *freely*, to turn to God or to turn away from God, to seek grace or avoid it, to be willing for our attachments to be lightened or to hold on to them.

To return to Augustine's metaphor, we may not be able to make our hands completely empty in order to receive the gifts of grace, but we can choose whether to relax our hands a little or to keep clenching them ever more tightly. In the face of significant addiction, our degree of choice may seem small; simply relaxing one's hands may seem too passive. As we shall see, however, this simple choice may be the greatest kind of struggle any human being can face, and it may call forth the greatest courage and dedication. There is nothing passive about it. In the long run, it may prove far more assertive and powerful than any other possible action we could take. It is, after all, the pure, naked aspiration of the human soul toward freedom and, through freedom, to love.

We may go through a great deal of humbling, if not outright humiliation, before we come to this simplicity of hope. We do not like admitting defeat, and we will struggle valiantly, even foolishly, to prove that we can master our destinies. God, in whose image we are made, instills in us the capacity for relentless tenacity, an assertiveness that complements our yearning hunger for God. But most of us overdo it; our spirit of assertiveness quickly becomes a spirit of pride. We will never really turn to God in loving openness as long as we are handling things well enough by ourselves. And it is precisely our most powerful addictions that cause us to defeat ourselves, that bring us to the rock bottom realization that we cannot finally master everything. Thus, although in one sense addiction is the enemy of grace, it can also be a powerful channel for the flow of grace. Addiction can be, and often is, the thing that brings us to our knees. Again the words of Paul are relevant:

I was given a painful wound to my pride, which came as Satan's messenger to bruise me. Three times I begged God to rid me of it, but God's answer was: "My grace is all you need; my power finds its full strength in weakness." Therefore I shall *prefer to find my joy and my pride in the things that are my weakness; and then the power of Christ will come and rest upon me.* For this reason I am content, for the sake of Christ, with weakness, contempt, persecution, hardship, and frustration; for when I am weak, then I am strong.[20]

Like Paul, it is possible that at some point on the journey with addiction and grace, we might even come to see addiction as a kind of gift. Some of the greatest spiritual authorities on addictions, the spiritual fathers and mothers of the Christian desert tradition, were emphatic about this. "Whoever has not experienced temptation cannot enter into the Reign of Heaven," said Abba Anthony. "Take away temptations and no one will be saved," said Evagrius. Addiction teaches us not to be too proud. Sooner or later, addiction will prove to us that we are not gods.[21]

Then we will realize that we are our own worst enemies; we cannot beat ourselves. At that point, when we have exhausted all the available false repositories for our hope, it is possible that we will turn to God with a true sense of who we are, with an integrity that is both humble and confident, with a dignity that knows itself because it has met its limits.[22]

Hope can sometimes be an elusive thing, and occasionally it must come to us with pain. But it is there, irrevocably. Like freedom, hope is a child of grace, and grace cannot be stopped. I refer once more to Saint Paul, a man who, I am convinced, understood addiction: "Hope will not be denied, because God's love has been poured into our hearts."[23]

2. EXPERIENCE: The Qualities of Addiction

It is the nature of desire not to be satisfied, and most human beings live only for the gratification of it.

ARISTOTLE

I could tell many stories as examples of how people experience addiction. I think of Sam, addicted to alcohol. He is fifty-eight but looks ninety because he has been drinking since he was a teenager. Once full of hope and dreams, he now languishes in a mental hospital. Doris, in contrast, leads an active and overtly successful life. She is socially popular and an effective businesswoman, but she is addicted to eating. Happy on the outside, she secretly hates herself because she cannot control her weight. Then there is Jim, a man of moderation in all things except his work. Addicted to his own sense of responsibility and the need to perform, he worries constantly about money and security. He is recovering from a heart attack, and his family hopes he will now slow down. He doubts that he can. I also think of Frank, a loving father and dedicated husband, who is completely entranced, compelled, by his infatuation with another woman. He was certain at first that the love he experienced was the purest he had ever known. Then, for a while, it seemed he was a slave of sexual desire. Now, as he longs for nothing other than freedom from both his wife and his lover, he has lost all understanding. He simply does not know what to do. And I remember Jean, a sweet and gracious homemaker. Jean is addicted to her relationship with her husband, who berates and belittles her at every opportunity. Friends who have witnessed this tell her to stand up to him, but the very thought of threatening the relationship fills her with panic.

These people's situations are not at all unusual, but they are extreme. Their addictions have crippled them over long periods of time and have severely corroded their self-esteem. My greatest interest, however, is the experience of ordinary, mundane addictions, the kind that all of us suffer. Perhaps the best way to begin to understand this experience is with an example of a temporary and simple chemical addiction.

The Addiction of a Nose

Sally had a summer cold. Her nose was runny, her eyes watered, and her throat was sore. At any other time, she would have let the cold run its course, but she had a vacation coming up, and she wanted to enjoy it. She talked her reluctant doctor into prescribing penicillin. She swallowed mounds of Vitamin C tablets and drank gallons of liquids. She also bought a large bottle of the strongest nose drops she could find.

The nose drops gave her dramatic, almost instantaneous, relief. Within seconds, she could breathe freely again. Three hours later the effects wore off. She could feel her nose starting to run again; it even seemed a little worse than before. So she used another dropperful. Again the effect was dramatic, but it only lasted a couple of hours. The next time she used two dropperfuls. Again it worked, but only for an hour. Each time she used the drops, their effects wore off more quickly, and her nose was stuffier than ever. Sally realized she was overdoing it, and several times she resolved to stop. But she made excuses to herself and kept on using the drops. She even got to the point of telling herself, "Just one more time."

The following day Sally had gone through most of the bottle and she couldn't breathe through her nose at all. The drops no longer had any effect whatsoever, and she was due to leave for the ocean the next day. Although she knew it was silly, she could think of nothing but her solidified nose. She had "forgotten" all about overdoing the nose drops and was now convinced she needed stronger ones, perhaps something available by prescription. She called her doctor, who scolded her for exceeding the recommended dosage and told her to stop the drops entirely. But Sally was feeling desperate. "I simply have to have something stronger!" she shouted. But the doctor refused and said to have faith; if she left her nose alone it would clear up in a day or two. Sally argued and pleaded, but the doctor remained adamant. Finally, angry but defeated, Sally had no choice but to leave her nose alone. It was not easy. At first her nose just seemed to get worse, and Sally became increasingly irritable and restless. As the doctor had predicted, however, everything cleared up after a couple of days, and Sally was finally able to enjoy her vacation. Sally says she will never use nose drops again.

This example of a temporary chemical attachment can teach us a great deal about the characteristics of addiction. Let us begin with the physiology. Virtually all body functions take place as a result of shifting *balances* among chemicals that have opposing effects. The body makes chemicals that stimulate the activity of glands and organs, and opposing chemicals that inhibit that activity. What actually happens in the body at a given time depends upon these balances. Nasal secretions are no exception. Certain natural body chemicals cause nasal congestion by increasing nasal secretion, while others cause decongestion by inhibiting secretion. The balance between these opposing natural chemicals determines the condition of one's nose.

The cold virus had caused irritation and an increase in natural congesting chemicals in Sally's nose. The nose drops contained decongestant chemicals, artificially made, but very much like the ones the body creates naturally. These artificial chemicals dried her nose up, but they also disturbed the natural balance. Trying to restore this balance, Sally's nose adjusted by producing more congesting chemicals and less of its own decongestants. Then, when the effect of the drops wore off, there were more natural congesting chemicals and less natural decongestants than there had been to start with, and therefore her nose was stuffier than ever. So she used more nose drops, and the vicious cycle continued until her nose was producing huge amounts of its own congestants and almost no decongestants at all. In trying to keep the balance, her nose had literally become *dependent* on the artificial decongestants in the drops. Her nose had become addicted. It had built up tolerance, needing more and more of the drops, and she had to put her nose through withdrawal symptoms before it could find its natural balance again.

This, in brief, is the way the body becomes addicted to substances. The substance alters a balance of natural body chemicals; the body adjusts to this alteration by trying to reestablish the proper balance. In so doing, the body becomes dependent upon the external supply of the substance. In the same way, people become addicted to stimulants, depressants, laxatives, narcotics, and a host of other substances.[1]

You will also note, however, that the struggle of Sally's nose was paralleled by a struggle in her mind, one that led to preoccupation, obsession, and even mild despair. Afterward, the whole thing seemed rather absurd to Sally—making such a big deal out of a stuffy nose—but at the time it seemed beyond her control. She had made stupid excuses and rationalizations to herself to justify her abuse of the drops. There was even a point, during that last conversation with the doctor, that she felt she almost could have killed for just one bottle of really powerful nose drops. In addition, she experienced a temporary but very real impairment of her opinion of herself and of her concern for other things and other people. Her little brush with addiction had not only wreaked havoc with her nose and made her play games with her mind, it had also eroded her freedom, her will, and her capacity for love. I will be discussing all these physical, psychological, and spiritual dynamics in greater detail, but at this point we can proceed to define addiction more precisely and establish its primary characteristics.

The Definition of Addiction

Addiction is any compulsive, habitual behavior that limits the freedom of human desire. It is caused by the attachment, or nailing, of desire to specific objects. The word *behavior* is especially important in this definition, for it indicates that *action* is essential to addiction. As I have indicated, attachment of desire is the underlying process that results in addictive behavior. In Sally's case, nose drops were the object of her attachment, but for her attachment to become true addiction, she had to act on it; she had to *use* the drops. Narcotic users imply this emphasis on behavior when they speak of "doing" drugs. When Sally finally stopped using the drops, even though she wanted them more than ever for a while, her addictive behavior had ceased. Shortly after that, the attachment itself began to lessen; she no longer felt a desire for the drops.

As we shall see, the relationship between attachment and addiction is not as simple as it might sound. For one thing, the brain never completely forgets its old attachments, so the absence of conscious desire does not necessarily mean attachment is gone. In fact, because of the tricks our minds play on us, many of our addictions are able to exist for years *completely outside our awareness;* it is only when our addictions are frustrated or cause us conflict that we have an opportunity to notice how attached we truly are.

Another complicating factor is that behavior is not limited to external physical activity. Thinking is also a behavior, a "doing." Thus images, memories, fantasies, ideas, concepts, and even certain feeling states can become objects of attachment, and one can become fully addicted to them. We have all experienced obsessive thoughts—the tune that repeatedly runs through the mind, the unrealistic worry that refuses to go away. Perhaps we have also recognized that there are certain images of ourselves or concepts about the world that we somehow feel deeply forced to hold on to. Some of us might even admit to having been addicted to certain moods—depression, shyness, cynicism, and the like.

With these additional considerations in mind, it is obvious that still more precision is needed to adequately understand the nature of addiction. We can take a significant step toward precision by exploring five essential characteristics that mark true addiction: (1) tolerance, (2) withdrawal symptoms, (3) self-deception, (4) loss of willpower, and (5) distortion of attention. We can use these five characteristics to determine areas of addiction within our own lives and to distinguish the slavery of addiction from the freedom of true caring.

Tolerance

Tolerance is the phenomenon of always wanting or needing more of the addictive behavior or the object of attachment in order to feel satisfied. What one has or does is never quite enough. Subjectively, the feeling might be something like, "If only I could get some more, everything would be fine." Typically, however, tolerance is not something that one is aware of; it happens insidiously. As in Sally's case, the body adjusts to the object of attachment by establishing a new chemical balance. This new balance diminishes the effect of the object. Thus Sally's nose produced more congestants to balance the artificial decongestants, and, as a result, Sally had to use more drops to get the desired effect.

The same process happens with nonsubstance addictions. Take my attachment to money as an example. To put it mildly, I have felt the need for more money at a number of points in my life. With time and work, I made more money. But then I adjusted to my improved standard of living, and I began to feel the need for still more. The essential dynamic of tolerance, then, is that one becomes used to a certain amount of something, and this accustomedness removes the desired effect and leads to the need for more.

Withdrawal Symptoms

Two types of withdrawal symptoms are experienced when an addictive behavior is curtailed. The first is a *stress reaction*. When the body is deprived of something it has become accustomed to, it responds with danger signals, as if something is wrong.

This response is mediated by the autonomic part of the nervous system, the part of the nervous system that deals with internal, automatic functions. It is not directly controllable by the conscious mind. Stress reactions may range from mild uneasiness and irritability to extreme agitation with rapid pulse, tremors, and overwhelming panic.

The second type of withdrawal symptom is a *rebound* or *backlash* reaction. The person experiences symptoms that are the exact opposite of those caused by the addictive behavior itself. Sally's nose demonstrated such a rebound when it became more congested after she stopped using the nose drops. Backlashes occur because the body's balancing mechanisms have become dependent on a particular substance or pattern of behavior. When that particular factor is suddenly removed, the balance swings in the opposite direction. Thus withdrawal from alcohol and other sedatives can produce hyperactivity and even seizures, while withdrawal from stimulants can result in lethargy, depression, and somnolence.

The situation with nonsubstance addictions is similar. If I am addicted to gaining other people's approval in order to feel good about myself, and if I have become accustomed to established ways of pleasing others, I will experience considerable stress in response to an outright rejection. I will also experience a rebound of feeling especially bad about myself.

Self-Deception

One of the most significant hallmarks of addiction is the exquisite inventiveness that the mind can demonstrate in order to perpetuate addictive behaviors. Here, where the will fights against itself in a morass of mixed motivations and contradictory desires, the creative power of the brain is used unconsciously to subvert each and every attempt to control the addictive behavior. These tricks of the mind include denial, rationalization, displacement, and every other defense mechanism that psychoanalysis has identified, plus a seemingly

endless variety of others that even the best psychiatric authorities could not predict. Mind tricks are so malignant, and have
such a corrosive effect upon self-esteem, that I will be discussing them at some length in the next chapter.

Loss of Willpower

As soon as one tries to control any truly addictive behavior
by making autonomous intentional resolutions, one begins to
defeat oneself. For the most part, defeat is due to mixed motivations. One part of the will sincerely wants to be free. Another
part wants to continue the addictive behavior. In any true addiction, the second part is stronger, and so the resolutions fail.
A fundamental mind trick of addiction is focusing attention on
willpower. In very complicated ways, the mind asserts that it in
fact can control the behavior. At certain points, it even encourages making resolutions to stop. It knows such resolutions are
likely to fail, and when they do, the addictive behavior will have
a stronger foothold than ever. It may take many such defeats
before one realizes how truly out of control one is.

Loss of willpower is especially important for defining the difference between the slavery of true addiction and the freedom
of sincerely caring about something or of choosing to satisfy
simple desires. If you find yourself saying, "I can handle it," "I
can stop it," or "I can do without it," try to perform a very
simple test: simply go ahead and stop it. Do without it. If you
are successful, there is no addiction. If you cannot stop, no
amount of rationalization will change the fact that addiction
exists.

Distortion of Attention

As I have indicated, we have many addictions we don't even
know about. The mind is often able to keep these addictions
hidden, even from ourselves, as long as we are getting a sufficient supply of the object of attachment and are experiencing

no great conflict about it. This does not, however, mean that our attention is free for other things. Addiction and its associated mind tricks inevitably kidnap and distort our attention, profoundly hindering our capacity for love. Attention and love are intimate partners; for love to be actualized, attention must be free.

It is easy to understand that the attention of a heroin addict seeking a fix will be wholly preoccupied with that specific task. There will be no room for attending to anything else. Human loving is out of the question. Truly desperate narcotic addicts can be capable of injuring and even killing themselves and others in the search for a fix. As I try to think of a milder, more universal example, I recall a recent trip to the grocery store. I was in a hurry, and the checkout line was long. Ahead of me, a mother tried to keep two tired children from fighting while she unloaded her cart. The clerk couldn't find the price of another person's item. My impatience completely usurped any thoughts of charity or compassion I might otherwise have had. For that moment, getting through the line quickly had become more important to me than anything else. We all are subject to such petty concerns, so much so that we become used to them. As I said, we seldom even recognize them as attachments.

In the great spiritual traditions of the world, attachments are seen as any concerns that usurp our desire for love, anything that becomes more important to us than God. Paul Tillich said that whatever we are ultimately concerned with is God for us. At any given moment, that with which we are most concerned is most likely to be something other than the true God. No matter how religious we may think we are, our addictions are always capable of usurping our concern for God. If we are worried about our financial status, that will become our ultimate concern at the time. The drama of a special human relationship may completely preoccupy our attention. Even things as simple as finding the right brand name for a purchase or discovering a scratch on our new car can, for a while, become ultimate concerns. From a religious standpoint, then, this distortion of attention, which is the fifth characteristic of addiction, could be called "the distortion of ultimate concern." Another word for it is idolatry.

Whether we are conscious of it or not, for however long a particular addiction controls our attention, it has become a god for us. The major religious traditions of the world proclaim in unison that such false gods must fall away from us. We are called to grow toward that point at which nothing other than God will be our god. However short-lived or minor our concern for something other than God may be, when we give it more priority than we give our concern for God and God's will, we commit idolatry. Thus we all commit idolatry countless times every day.

These are harsh words. Some of us who call ourselves religious might wish to maintain that although we may *appear* to be more concerned with this or that superficial thing, at some underlying existential level we are still *really* most concerned with God. Our most immediate concern, we might claim, is not the same thing as our ultimate concern. But even a brief honest examination quickly reveals the lie. All we need is to look at our actions; while claiming to be loving God, we are in fact living our addictions. These words not only seem harsh; they may also sound familiar. Similar things have been repeated for centuries from a multitude of pulpits: "You, who call yourselves faithful, do not live in accord with what you say you believe." The theme is almost trite, because the problem is universal.

Too often, sermons on idolatry simply leave people feeling guilty. It is true that we are responsible for our actions, and in that sense we are indeed guilty of being more concerned with our addictions than with love. But to stop there is to assume we can eradicate our attachments through willpower alone, and we simply cannot. Those of us who have tried to change our addictions (and at one time or another most all of us have) know it is not so easy. But it achieves nothing to heap guilt upon ourselves; it only makes us even more self-preoccupied.

Instead, I think we need to keep in mind two important things that the experience of addiction and grace can teach us.

First, although God calls us all *toward* more perfect life, we cannot personally achieve the *state* of perfection. We can and should do our very best to move in that direction, struggling with every resource we have, but we must also accept the reality of our incompleteness. Second, we need to recognize that the incompleteness within us, our personal insufficiency, does not make us unacceptable in God's eyes. Far from it; our incompleteness is the empty side of our longing for God and for love. It is what draws us toward God and one another. If we do not fill our minds with guilt and self-recriminations, we will recognize our incompleteness as a kind of spaciousness into which we can welcome the flow of grace. We can think of our inadequacies as terrible defects, if we want, and hate ourselves. But we can also think of them affirmatively, as doorways through which the power of grace can enter our lives. Then we may begin to appreciate our inherent, God-given lovableness.[2]

Security Addictions

The presence of addiction should be suspected whenever interior human freedom is compromised. As I said, the five characteristics of addiction can be used to identify areas of addiction in our own lives and to distinguish these addictions from free desires and love. As an example, let us look at the universal human search for security. Even the most well adjusted or spiritually mature of us can identify some addictions within this arena of life.

The monotheistic religions are unequivocal in stating that we can and should trust in God for our ultimate security. Jesus even went so far as to say we need not worry about possessions or practical needs for the future. Our real call, he said, is to be concerned with God; we are free to do this because we can trust God's grace to take care of the rest of our needs. The same beautiful theme of human freedom has followed us since the beginning. In the context of our needs for security, however, we begin to see the price of this freedom.[3]

Freedom and security have always been uneasy together; the things that secure us tend to bind us down, and those that free us often feel like risks. We are meant to be free enough to really love God and one another, but true freedom can happen only if we completely trust in God's ultimate care for us. And to really trust God, we must begin to relax our grip and ease our concern about all the lesser sources of security to which we have become attached. This can feel risky indeed.

Little in our normal life supports really trusting God. All around us we see bad things happening to people, and, at least on our terms, God may not seem trustworthy at all. Our culture communicates that truly putting oneself in God's hands is superstitious, irresponsible, even psychotic. "In God We Trust" may be inscribed on American money, but the money itself usually feels more trustworthy. In this world of daily experience, Jesus' words about the lilies of the field can sound naive, even dangerous. Few if any of us are able to follow Jesus' call for trust completely.

Instead, we assume that trust in God should be only a spiritual ideal, wistfully and distantly respected, but impossible to apply in the down-to-earth conduct of our daily lives. True spiritual freedom, we maintain, is something that we can consider *after* we have established our physical and relational security in the world. In our culture, the three gods we do trust for security are possessions, power, and human relationships. To a greater or lesser extent, all of us worship this false trinity.

In the realm of possessions, we try to acquire and hold on to sufficient income and property. This is what we call financial security, and we hope it will eventually provide us and our heirs with freedom and peace of mind. We would even say that a certain degree of financial security is essential for us to go about our other good works in the world, because without it we would have to spend all our time taking care of our own needs. To some extent, this makes sense. But most often the acquisition of money and possessions leads to less freedom and more worry. When we can see our freedom impaired, we should consider the presence of addiction.

In the arena of power, we seek status, influence, and control over our lives. In part this relates to financial security, but it also includes claiming and holding self-determination and autonomy in the face of the many forces around us. The more personal power we have, the less vulnerable we feel. When we use the word *freedom* in a social or political context, we are normally referring to this capacity to secure our self-interests. Again, to a certain extent, the actions are reasonable. But although self-determining autonomy can indeed free us from being oppressed by other people, it is often overdone. It easily becomes egotistical and selfish. Then, instead of serving freedom, autonomy forces us to bow down before the idol of our own will. Here again is a sign of addiction.

In terms of human relationships, we try to secure both short-term affiliations and long-term bonds with other people. Ideally, relationships are the vehicle through which we most directly love and are loved. Relationships can also provide us with feelings of personal worth, value, and affirmation. They are a central source of connectedness and love, of stability and solidity in our lives. Much of the time relationships serve our freedom as individuals and the freedom of the larger communities of which we are a part.[4]

But relationships can also tyrannize us. We may become too dependent or too possessive. We may manipulate or be manipulated. Our sense of personal worth, goodness, or lovability may become contingent on the approval of others. It is likely that addiction is present when such things happen, because freedom is compromised. Our personal worth and value, our capacity to love and be loved, and our ultimate care and protection are all things that have been given to us by God as our birthrights. When we feel bound to extract these qualities from other people, something is wrong.[5]

Everyone in our culture seeks some kind of security within the realms of possessions, power, and relationships. By asking ourselves questions about our experience with these three areas and the five characteristics of addiction, we can see what serves freedom and what is addiction. Very simply, addiction exists wherever we can find evidence of all five of the characteristics.

If I were still denying my own addictive behavior I would not want to answer the following questions. As it is, I accept the fact that I am well and truly addicted in all three areas. To assist my acceptance, I like to remember that my incompleteness can be a space for grace. I also appreciate God's words to Paul: "My grace is all you need; my power finds its full strength in weakness."

First, some questions that might reveal *tolerance:*

—Do I feel that the amount of money and possessions I have right now is sufficient for my security, or do I feel I'd really be better off with more?
—Is my sense of power and control sufficient, or do I feel I need more?
—Are the important people in my life reliable, understanding, and loving enough, or would I feel more secure if they were more so?

Second, some questions about *withdrawal symptoms:*

—How do I feel if someone or something threatens to take away my possessions, power, or relationships?
—In a typical week, how much time, worry, and energy do I spend trying to hold on to these things?
—If I were to lose one or more of them, how would I feel?
—In the past, when I have suffered such losses, did I experience the stress reaction of withdrawal (anxiety, physical agitation, tremulousness, irritability, and so on)?
—Have I experienced the backlash or rebound reactions of withdrawal (feelings of deep *in*security, an "end-of-the-world" kind of vulnerability)?

Third, some questions about *self-deception:*

—Do I ever find myself making excuses, denials, or playing other mind tricks to rationalize acquiring more possessions or power or to justify destructive behaviors in relationships?
—Have there been occasions when I've wanted to hide some of my possessions from others or to disclaim my power because I really think I have too much?
—Have I sometimes just discovered myself caught up in some security-seeking behavior that I would never have chosen if I'd had my wits about me?
—Have friends or family reflected that they think I'm more attached to some of these things than I myself feel I am?
—Do I sometimes have trouble settling down for quiet reflection, perhaps because I don't want to confront my own truth about these things?
—Have I ever found myself thinking "I can take it or leave it" or "I can handle it" in relation to possessions, power, or relationships?

Fourth, questions about *loss of willpower:*

—Have I ever made any resolutions to ease the importance I give to possessions, power, or relationships?
—Have I felt success or failure, pride or defeat with these resolutions, and what were the consequences of those feelings?
—Have I resolved, for example, to contribute more to charity or to be more giving than receiving or to avoid certain kinds of relationships, only to find myself behaving in the same old ways?
—Have I ever gotten to the point with any of these areas where my feelings changed from simple desires to real compulsion, a demanding need that truly seemed out of my control?

Fifth, a question about *distortion of attention:*

—Where and when do my concerns about possessions, power, or relationships kidnap my attention and eclipse my concern for:
—love of God?
—love of others?
—love of myself?

Attraction and Aversion Addictions

Thus far, I have been speaking of addiction as if it always draws us toward something that attracts us. But addictions, and their underlying attachments, need not necessarily be to things we find pleasurable. Desire has two sides; its dark side is repulsion. Just as we may be compulsively drawn toward some things, we are compulsively pushed away from others. There are things we can't stand, things we are afraid of, people we can't abide. Often, our repulsions too take on the characteristics of addiction. Thus, in addition to the *attraction* addictions we have been discussing, we must also consider *aversion* addictions. We often call repulsions by other names: phobias, prejudices, bigotries, resistances, or allergies.[6]

Sometimes an aversion addiction is simply an attraction addiction stated in reverse. For example, if I am addicted to cleanliness, who is to say whether I am basically drawn toward neatness or repelled by dirt? Other aversion addictions, however, exist absolutely in their own right. This is particularly true of racial, ethnic, or sexual prejudices, and of many phobias. One of the most physically dangerous aversion addictions is anorexia nervosa. This compulsive avoidance of food can be even more life threatening than alcoholism.

As we shall see, the dynamics of aversion addictions are essentially mirror images of those of attraction addictions. Instead of tolerance, where we can't get enough of a thing, we experience *in*tolerance, where no matter how little of a thing we have, it is still too much. Instead of withdrawal symptoms, the distress we experience when we lose something, there are *approach* symptoms, feelings of panic, fear, or disgust when we get too close to that which we abhor. The other characteristics that we have listed apply equally to aversion addictions.

Examples of Addictions

Prior to writing this book, I conducted several workshops in which a large number of people used these five characteristics to identify addictions in many different areas of their lives. I kept a list of these addictions, and I will share it with you now as a way of demonstrating how wide ranging and pervasive addiction can be (Tables 2–1 and 2–2).

Because virtually anything in life can become an object of attachment, it is especially important to remember that there is a big difference between having strong feelings about something and really being addicted to it. The difference is freedom. We care deeply about many things and abhor many others, but with most of these we remain free to choose the depth and extent of our investment. They do not become gods. Remember, then, that true addictions are compulsive habitual behaviors that eclipse our concern for God and compromise our freedom, and that they must be characterized by tolerance, withdrawal symptoms, loss of willpower, and distortion of attention.

Some of these addictions are tragic, others are humorous, and some may seem completely absurd. But they are all real for someone, and, taken together, they provide a spectrum within which, I suspect, you can find something that applies to yourself. I am sure you will be able to add your own unique contributions to these lists. If it is any consolation, I am addicted to at least fourteen of the listed items, and I could add several others if I wanted to be completely candid, which I do not.

Aren't There Some Good Addictions?

Having looked over tables 2–1 and 2–2, one might be prompted to ask whether all addictions must be seen as negative.

Table 2-1: ATTRACTION ADDICTIONS

Anger	Drinking	Intimacy	Relationships
Approval	Drugs	Jealousy	Responsibility
Art	Eating	Knowledge	Revenge
Attractiveness	Envy	Lying	Scab picking
Being good	Exercise	Marriage	Seductiveness
Being helpful	Fame	Meeting	Self-image
Being loved	Family	expectations	Self-improve-
Being nice	Fantasies	Memories	ment
Being right	Finger	Messiness	Sex
Being taken	drumming	Money	Shoplifting
care of	Fishing	Movies	Sleeping
Calendars	Food	Music	Soft drinks
Candy	Friends	Nail biting	Sports
Cars	Furniture	Neatness	Status
Causes	Gambling	Parents	Stock market
Chewing gum	Gardening	Performance	Stress
Children	Golf	Pets	Sunbathing
Chocolate	Gossiping	Pimple squeezing	Suspiciousness
Cleanliness	Groups	Pistachio nuts	Talking
Coffee	Guilt	Pizza	Television
Comparisons	Hair twisting	Politics	Time
Competence	Happiness	Popcorn	Tobacco
Competition	Hobbies	Popularity	Weight
Computers	Housekeeping	Potato chips	Winning
Contests	Humor	Power	Work
Death	Hunting	Psychotherapy	Worthiness
Depression	Ice cream	Punctuality	
Dreams	Images of God	Reading	

Couldn't some of them be beneficial? What about a mother's "addiction" to her children? A husband's "attachment" to his wife? Or, for that matter, the spiritual person's "attachment" to God? Might it not be constructive to be attractionally addicted to some of the good things in life and aversionally addicted to the bad? After all, aren't there good habits as well as bad ones?

Table 2–2: AVERSION ADDICTIONS

Airplanes	Commitment	Mice	Public speaking
Anchovies	Conflict	Needles	Rats
Anger	Crowds	Open spaces	Rejection
Animals	Darkness	Pain	Responsibility
Being:	Death	People of	Sex
Abnormal	Dentists	different:	Sharp instruments
Alone	Dependence	Beliefs	Slimy creatures
Discounted	Dirt	Class	Snakes
Fat	Disapproval	Culture	Spiders
Judged	Doctors	Politics	Storms
Over-	Embarrassment	Race	Strangers
whelmed	Evil spirits	Religion	Success
Thin	Failure	Sex	Tests
Tricked	Fire	People who are:	Traffic
Birds	Germs	Addicted	Tunnels
Blood	Guilt	Competent	Vulnerability
Boredom	High places	Fat/Thin	Water
Bridges	Illness	Ignorant	Writing
Bugs	Independence	Neat/Messy	
Cats	Intimacy	Rich/Poor	
Closed-in			
spaces			

Such questions bring us into one of the most difficult territories we must cross in our exploration of addiction and grace, for the answer is as unequivocal as it is unpleasant; *no* addiction is good; *no* attachment is beneficial. To be sure, some are more destructive than others; alcoholism cannot be compared with chocolate addiction in degrees of destructiveness, and fear of spiders pales in comparison to racial bigotry. But if we accept that there are differences in the degree of tragedy imposed upon us by our addictions, we must also recognize what they have in common: they impede human freedom and diminish the human spirit.

It is surely good for parents to care for their children and for people to be kind to one another and to seek God. It would be wonderful if we could make a habit of such activities. But there is a vast difference between doing these things because we freely choose and doing them because we are compelled. In the first case, the motivation is love; in the second, slavery.

One could make the case that motivation is not so important, that what counts is getting the good things done. In short-term situations this seems to make sense. Some good things *are* done because of addiction. If someone is hungry, it is indeed better that they be fed by someone who is attached to doing good deeds than that they starve because someone else is "free" to choose not to feed them. But consider this hypothetical second person for a moment. If he or she were really free from attachment, there would be no reason *not* to feed the hungry one. Love, the core of our creation, would call it forth spontaneously. The only reason we could have for "choosing" against true compassion and charity is that we are addicted to something else. Uncharitable behavior can never be justified on the basis of freedom from attachment; to try to do so is to engage in mind tricks, not freedom.

Further, the entire situation posed here is irrevocably hypothetical, for no one is truly free from attachment. We must work with our addictions, seeking the grace within them and trying to minimize their destructiveness instead of spending our time fantasizing what it would be like to be totally free of them. Total freedom, religion tells us, is paradise—the final salvation and the full reign of God. It is a goal that we must work toward, but it is also something we must hope and wait for. Paul speaks of this in words that we will hear again in our exploration of addiction and grace: "From the beginning till now, all creation has been groaning in one great act of giving birth; we too groan inwardly as we wait for our bodies to be set free. . . . It is something we must wait for in patience."[7]

No, we must try to put to rest any notion that addictions are good. The only goodness in them is that they can defeat our pride and lead us to more openness to grace. It may also help to remember that the destructiveness of addiction does not lie in the things to which we are attached, nor even in our simple desires for them. The things themselves are simply part of creation, and God made them inherently good. The destructiveness of addiction lies in our *slavery* to these things, turning desire into compulsion, with ugly and loveless consequences for ourselves and our world. The more we can understand about how enslavement happens to us, the more we may be able to turn in the direction of freedom and love.[8]

3. MIND: The Psychological Nature of Addiction

> There is a general tendency of our mental apparatus . . . it seems to find expression in the tenacity with which we hold on to the sources of pleasure at our disposal, and in the difficulty with which we renounce them.
>
> SIGMUND FREUD

Addiction attacks every part of what Freud called our "mental apparatus." Subjectively, however, the attacks seem focused on two primary areas: the will, which is our capacity to choose and direct our behavior, and self-esteem, which is the respect and value with which we view ourselves. Addiction splits the will in two, one part desiring freedom and the other desiring only to continue the addictive behavior. This internal inconsistency begins to erode self-esteem. How much can I respect myself if I do not even know what I really want?

The greatest damage to self-esteem, however, comes from repeated failures at trying to change addictive behavior. Even if I do feel clear about what I really want, I cannot make myself behave accordingly. I seem to be honestly out of control; yet, in all truth, I have only myself to blame. This failure can decimate my self-respect. In some other culture, in a society that reveres the mystery of human nature more than ours does, such failures at self-mastery might not be so devastating. They might even be seen as affirmations of one's essential connectedness with the rest of creation and of one's essential dependency upon the Creator. But in modern Western society, we have come to see ourselves as objects of our own creation. When we fail at managing ourselves, we feel defective.

The best way to understand this devastation of will and self-esteem is to examine the actual experience of people who have suffered from major chemical addiction. The mind's battle to deceive itself, with all its insidious tricks and strategies, can be fully appreciated only by people who have suffered such life-threatening addictions. Yet, as they describe their experience, we sense something with which we can all identify. It is as if these severely addicted people have played out, on an extreme scale, a drama that all human beings experience more subtly and more covertly.

Self-Deception

As I discuss some of the mind tricks occurring in major chemical addiction, remember that they all have a single purpose: to keep the addictive behavior going. Also note that they do not necessarily occur in the progressive order in which I present them. They overlap with one another and repeat themselves in a vicious cycle of self-deceit. We begin with the two most primitive and universal defense mechanisms described by Freudian psychology, denial and repression.

Denial and Repression

During the early stages of the development of chemical addiction, the conscious mind studiously ignores or rejects any signs of increasing use of the substance. Not only does the person not recognize that a problem exists, she doesn't want to think about it. She doesn't see any reason even to consider it. This is denial. Evidence for addiction may be perfectly obvious to other people, but it is as if the addicted person is either completely blind to it or always looking in another direction. As evidence mounts, however, the addicted person must use increasing psychological energy to keep the truth out of his awareness. This is the beginning of repression. Somewhere deep inside, the person now recognizes that addiction exists, but he keeps the knowledge unconscious. Not only does this take considerable energy; it also means the person cannot be comfortable with himself. He must always keep his mind either occupied or dulled, so that no clear space opens within which the conscious realization might occur. Moments of peaceful openness and self-reflection, which may have seemed so pleasant in the past, are now actively avoided. Prayer, meditation, and simple times of quiet relaxation are either discontinued or filled with activities that will occupy attention.

A therapist friend recently told me he had observed that "addicted people can't meditate." I agreed that chemically addicted people do indeed seem to have trouble settling down and being wakefully present, but I also had to add, "Don't we all sometimes find it difficult to relax with ourselves?" I know my own daily practice of prayer and meditation is not easy. One reason is that this practice opens my awareness to things about myself that I would rather not be conscious of. In many instances, these awarenesses have to do with my addictions: how attached I am to certain petty concerns and competitions, how worried I am about truly insignificant things, how important my selfish ego is to me. So I find myself resisting settling down to pray, or I fill my meditation time with images or music or words— anything that will keep me from simply being present and awake before God.

In major chemical addictions, times that once had this quality of open relaxed presence now often become occasions for using the addictive drug. In a sinister but perfect irony, the drug becomes its own camouflage; its effects cloud and alter awareness sufficiently to prevent realization of the person's addiction to it.

This pattern of denial and repression breeds a sense of alienation from oneself. One will do almost anything to avoid being present to oneself. Next one experiences a real fear of having nothing to do, a phobia of boredom, a dread of being alone with nothing to occupy one's attention. As with any phobia, the more one avoids such situations, the more terrifying they seem to become.

If a hint of the truth of the addiction should find its way into awareness, either through an unguarded moment of self-reflection or because another person points it out, other mechanisms come into play. The addicted person will change the subject, reject it out of hand, or conveniently forget to pursue it. The denial and repression can continue for life. It is not at all unusual to hear aged alcoholics, who have lost jobs, families, and homes, and who are now hospitalized with advanced cirrhosis of the liver, saying, "Hell, no. I've never had any trouble with booze. I can take it or leave it."

Rationalization

Wherever denial and repression fail, the addicted person realizes some kind of problem exists. The realization calls forth a new defensive maneuver, which is to rationalize, to make excuses in an attempt to justify the addictive behavior. These rationalizations are not intentional lies; the person actually tries to convince herself that they are true. "I need a drink because I feel depressed." "I deserve a drink to celebrate." "I have to have these pills to help me sleep." "Life is short, why not enjoy it?"

The very occurrence of such rationalizations is irrefutable evidence that addiction is present, for if there were no addiction, there would be no reason to make excuses. The addicted person recognizes this at some level, and rationalizing actually increases his internal distress and self-alienation. Once again, growing discomfort becomes the occasion for increasing the addictive behavior. The chemical now becomes a tranquilizer for the psychic distress it itself is causing.

Hiding

At some point, it becomes impossible to continue avoiding the truth. The addicted person knows full well that she has a real problem. Denial, repression, and rationalization do not necessarily stop; they simply fail to keep the truth hidden. The mechanisms continue and take on even more unrealistic proportions. But since hiding the truth from oneself is no longer as effective, it becomes increasingly important to hide it from other people. Now the addictive behavior becomes more secretive; the person may hide bottles and consciously lie. In addition to self-alienation, he experiences a growing isolation from other people. There is a sense of harboring a dark secret, the revelation of which would be unbearable. Although self-esteem has been being subtly eroded all along in this process, now a depressive, guilty, self-disparaging atmosphere pervades nearly everything the person does. To compensate, the addicted person may put on masks of competence, lightheartedness, and good humor. His charades can be very effective at fooling others, but internally they only intensify feelings of inadequacy and lack of integrity.

Delaying Tactics

In virtually every major addiction, there comes a time when one resolves to master it. The addicted person decides to quit. "I've really got to stop. I just need a little more discipline and willpower." Sensing an impending frontal attack upon its addiction, the mind comes up with the most cunning, inventive strategies possible. The more creative and intelligent the person, the more agonizing this process will be.

The mind will suggest, perhaps, that it is not wise to rush into such things. "I need to think this through and decide carefully when and how to quit and what my reasons and strategies will be." If this delaying tactic works, the mind can simply forget what it planned to think about. Then, when the memory does come back, the delay can happen again. "I simply *must* figure out how I am going to stop." The "resolving to resolve" stage can effectively prohibit any real action from taking place for years at a time.

Other procrastinations include looking for an ideal time to stop. "I'll wait until Lent; it would be a good spiritual discipline." "I can't stop yet because it will make me anxious and irritable for a while, and I have all this important work to attend to." "I'm really not feeling well enough right now." "Maybe I should pray about it and God will show me when and how to quit." "The next time I have a blackout, that will be the sign that it's time to quit." The mind is infinitely ingenious at *complicating* the process of quitting. When what is needed is direct, clear-cut refusal to perform the addictive behavior, the mind invents such convoluted and entangled complications that the addicted person finds himself thrashing about helplessly in an ocean of details.

After a while, the person may recognize some of these delaying tactics for what they are. But they are never *all* recognized, for the mind is endlessly inventive; it always has another, more subtle trick up its sleeve. Even when the person realizes that it is time to "put up or shut up," the delays continue. Of necessity, they also become more ludicrous. "Tomorrow. Tomorrow is D-Day. Tomorrow I'll quit." "Just one more fix, and that will be the last." "What I'll do is go and drink and drink until I get sick of it, and then I'll really want to quit." "Well, this is it. I'm going to quit. This is the red-letter day. I'll have a drink to celebrate."

If the person makes it through these deceptions to the point of authentically deciding to quit, a profound sense of terror will arise at the prospect of relinquishing the addictive behavior. On the surface, the fear will seem reasonable; the addiction has become so much a part of the person's life that its relinquishment feels like death. But it is just another mind trick, another delaying tactic. The truth, of course, is that the person survived quite well before the addiction and could do so again.

"I Can't Handle It"

Repeatedly failed resolutions eventually lead to depression and to some kind of admission of defeat. Failure may take either a passive or an aggressive form, both of which help to continue the addiction. In a passive response to defeat, the addicted person is besieged with feelings of shame, remorse, and guilt. This self-hatred may lead to suicidal impulses, but more often the person simply surrenders to the addiction. "I give up. I can't handle it, and I'm too tired to even go on fighting. All I can do is accept my addiction and go on drinking." There may be some grace in this admission of defeat, but it is still misperceived by the addicted person. If the person is sophisticated in the language of Alcoholics or Narcotics Anonymous, she is likely to try to convince herself that this, finally, is the rock-bottom surrender that will somehow save her. But the "higher power" to which she is surrendering is not God; it is the addiction itself.

The more aggressive response to repeated failure says, "To hell with it." This embittered, cynical reaction still has a depressive quality, but it seeks to preserve some vestiges of self-respect by bringing everything in life down to its own sense of worthlessness. "Yeah, I may be no good, but neither is anything else." "Who cares? What difference does it make?" "It's not worth it. I'm going to do whatever I want because nothing really matters anyway." When performed with finesse, such negativity can convince the addicted person that he is engaging in revolutionary rhetoric or philosophical nihilism. But, just like the passive response, it is simply another ploy to continue the addiction.

"I Can Handle It"

If, instead of failing, the person temporarily succeeds in stopping the addictive behavior, the greatest mind trick of all comes into play. It starts out very normally, with the natural joyfulness of liberation. "I can do it! I have done it! And it wasn't even that difficult! Why, I actually don't even have any desire for a drink anymore. I'm free!" Before long, the natural joy will undergo a malignant change; it will be replaced by pride.

The fall begins, in a day or a week or a few months, with the recurrence of an impulse to have a drink or a fix. It comes subtly and innocuously, certainly not as a conscious desire to resume the whole pattern of addictive behavior, just to engage in it once. Sometimes the desire appears unconscious. "I don't know what happened, I honestly don't. Everything was going so well, and I wasn't even thinking about drinking, but all of a sudden there I was, with a drink in my hand, and I was already feeling high." The downfall can seem for all the world like a demonically mystical happening. "It was as if there were another person inside of me I didn't even know was there. All the time I was feeling so good about my success, he was in there waiting for the chance to take over. And in a moment when I wasn't looking and my guard was down, he did." More often, the desire to have a drink, a pill, or a snort just gently surfaces in awareness, like a harmless little notion. "A drink would sure taste good right now." "Boy, if I weren't straight, this would sure be the time to get high." Or it may come more philosophically: "I haven't had a single pill for three weeks now. I wonder what it would be like. I bet it would be different now that I have no desire for it and I'm no longer hooked on it."

These impulses have a subtle but exceedingly important effect upon the person's feeling of success. The joyful sense of "I'm free" is changing to "I can handle it." For a while, "I can handle it" means the person feels she can fight off any impulses to engage in the addictive behavior. Before long, however, "I can handle it" means she thinks she can engage in the addictive behavior without becoming enslaved to it again. People have even been known to have a drink to celebrate their success at stopping drinking. The brilliance of this masterful mind trick is now evident; the pure joy of success and freedom has been transformed into an excuse for renewed failure and enslavement.

Even after the failure occurs, one can continue to believe one is somehow handling it. "I'm moderating it." "No more than three snorts a day." "I only drink on social occasions where it would be embarrassing to say no." "I only have one drink before supper." "I take a pill or two only on weekends." "It's not the occasional beer that gets me in trouble, it's the hard stuff." On and on the tactics go, until, again, it becomes painfully obvious that one is not handling it at all. Wherever "I can handle it" surfaces, the fall follows.

Breakdown

The fall is tragic in the classical sense, an abject crashing down after the pinnacles of pride have been attained. Once recognized, it brings guilt, remorse, and shame in bitter proportion to the pride that preceded it. Self-respect disappears. Suicide is considered. Without even the will to resist, the use of the chemical increases dramatically, further impairing judgment. A critically dangerous situation results. Through the haze of intoxication and depression, the mind continues its battle with itself. Increasingly bizarre forms of rationalization and resolution surface—forms that are possible only because the person's reason has been cruelly eroded. Other drugs are used to substitute for the primary substance, and secondary addictions develop. Desperately seeking a way out, unrealistic schemes are hatched. "If I could just get a hundred thousand dollars, my life would be different." "I'm going to leave everything and start life all over again in another country." These grow into proportions that can only be called psychotic. "If it weren't for my boss treating me the way he did, I wouldn't be in this state. He doesn't deserve to live." "It's a lousy, rotten world anyway. Who cares what I do? I'll show them I'm somebody." "It's all a matter of radio waves and vitamins. I'll eat lots of vitamins and figure out some way to hide from the radio waves."

Fortunately, not all major chemical addictions progress to this degree of devastation. But all of our addictions, even our nonsubstance addictions, share similar dynamics. And the most serious of our nonsubstance addictions even share a similarly ominous potential. Addiction to power, money, or relationships can drive people to distort reality just as much as can addiction to alcohol or narcotics.

Collusion

The mind tricks of addiction share yet another quality: they are contagious. No matter how much it may be kept hidden, addiction is never a completely individual thing. From the very first stages of the attachment process, other people are involved. Friends, family, coworkers, and even professional helpers affect and are affected by changes happening within the addicted person. Nearly always, some of their involvement helps to support the addiction. Their unwitting collusion has been well publicized in recent literature; it is called *codependency.* Codependency is not simply a matter of other people trying to cope with the addicted person's behavior. They actually create their own interweaving webs of deception. They may even unconsciously develop new, more inventive mind tricks for the addicted person to use. Ironically, it is the most sympathetic, compassionate, loving persons in the addict's social circle that are most likely to fall into such collusion.

Professional medical or psychological helpers are by no means immune to this problem. Physicians may prescribe other drugs to help people quit the primary chemical, thus producing multiple chemical addictions. Psychotherapeutic help may prolong the addictive behavior while therapist and client spend months or years trying to uncover nonexistent childhood experiences to explain the addiction. It is as if the therapist teaches the addicted person to think, "I have become addicted because of some personality defect or old psychological trauma. I must spend months, perhaps years, trying to identify and solve my psychological problems (and while all this goes on, I have an excuse to keep on being addicted)."

From the standpoint of the addicted person, all the mind tricks and self-deceptions have one dedicated purpose: to continue the addictive behavior. Likewise, there is only one dedicated action that really counteracts addiction, and that is to stop the addictive behavior. When the community surrounding an addicted person tries to help in any way that does not support ending the addiction, it will wind up supporting the addiction instead.

If we cut through all the camouflage and false complexities that addiction creates, we come back to the fundamental issue of contradictory motivations. At one level, both the chemically addicted person and his or her immediate community know that the taking of the chemical simply has to stop. Both the person and the community truly desire this. But at another, more insidious level of desire, they find themselves colluding with the addiction.

For the addicted person alone, struggling only with willpower, the desire to continue the addiction will win. It will win because it resides, as we shall see, at the level of biological conditioning, and it is always operative. Willpower and resolutions come and go, but the addictive process never sleeps. The caring community around the person has more potential than this. Even though this community is bound to have its own mind tricks and mixed motivations, it has a chance for a better perspective. Most importantly, the people who care about a chemically addicted person have one another. Grace is always a present possibility for individuals, but its flow comes to fullness through community. Grace flows toward appreciating the truth, toward an accurate understanding of what is going on beneath the confused surface of addiction. During the first third of this century, Sigmund Freud and his followers laid the foundations for such an understanding.

Psychoanalytic Insights

Freud, Jung, and other psychoanalysts proposed that all mental activity was fueled by a psychic energy they called *libido*. The exact nature of this energy was never made clear. Freud saw it as physical and sexual in nature, while Jung described it in more metaphysical terms. Both agreed, however, that psychic energy is invested in the activities, things, or persons that are especially important to an individual at a given time. The Greek word for this investment of energy is *cathexis*, literally meaning "holding." Freud's original German word was *besetzung*, meaning "being occupied with." According to psychoanalytic theory, then, cathexis is the investment of psychic energy through which we hold on to or occupy ourselves with whatever is important to us. Obviously, cathexis is the psychological equivalent of spiritual attachment.

Freud felt that our cathexes were determined by two dynamics: the pleasure principle and the reality principle. He saw pleasure principle motivations as seeking quick pleasure or immediate relief from distress: "I want what I want when I want it." In contrast, he felt decisions based on the reality principle required postponement of gratification in favor of more long-range or altruistic endeavors. In the light of modern behavioral psychology, Freud's pleasure and reality principles may seem outmoded. But they established pleasure and relief of pain as important determinants of behavior, thus laying a foundation for the motivational psychology that was to follow.

Psychoanalysts were also quick to point out that many significant cathexes occur *unconsciously*. The mind uses denial, repression, and a host of other defense mechanisms to keep us unaware of the truth of our motivations or to justify them falsely. For example, while I may know that much of my psychic energy is currently invested in writing this book well and clearly, I may not realize that some of the same energy is also invested in less admirable motives like trying to impress or compete with my colleagues. In terms of the spiritual life, we may think we are seeking to love God with purity of heart, but quite different and even conflicting motivations are normally present beneath awareness. Perhaps we are also trying to build a holy image of ourselves or to meet the expectations of others or to earn higher favor in the eyes of our image of God.

From a psychoanalytic standpoint, then, our unconscious motivations keep us from true purity of heart. We are not alone in the struggle. The writings of spiritual giants throughout history reveal their repeated struggles to find purity of heart and wholeness of love in the midst of their own mixed motivations. Further, as they grew in purity, they became ever more humbled by the apparent endlessness of their attachments. This is one reason why authentic spiritual growth is accompanied by increasing awareness of one's own need for God's mercy rather than pride in one's holiness. It may also be why Jesus revered the simple honesty of the tax collector's prayer: "God be merciful to me, a sinner."[1]

To summarize, psychoanalytic psychology has contributed the following important insights toward our understanding addiction: attachments form through the investment (cathexis) of psychic energy in certain activities, things, or people that bring us pleasure or relief from distress; many of these cathexes are kept unconscious by means of self-deception, so our motivations are never completely pure and may be quite contradictory.

The Myth of the Addictive Personality

In my opinion, at least one psychoanalytic theory pertaining to addiction has proven more harmful than helpful. This is the concept of the addictive personality. In brief, it assumes that chemical addictions occur because of preexisting personality defects. Early researchers observed that chemically addicted people seemed to operate on the basis of the pleasure principle. Addicted people were called "narcissistic," self-centered, manipulative, and devious, and they suffered from low self-esteem. The researchers concluded that some deep neurotic problem was responsible for the onset of addiction.

When I began working with substance abuse, I noted that addicted people did indeed tend to have little self-respect, and they often seemed manipulative, devious, and self-centered. At first I agreed that these were symptoms of an addiction-prone personality disorder. If that were the case, however, the symptoms should have been apparent before the addiction ever began. But detailed histories revealed no supporting evidence. Some people had become addicted as a result of seeking chemical relief from anxiety, depression, or other physical and emotional distress. Most, however, seemed to have led relatively normal lives before the addiction started. They had been capable of authentic respect for themselves, and in their dealings with others they had demonstrated compassion, honesty, and straightforwardness.

I had to conclude that the symptoms of addictive personality were caused *by* the addiction, not the cause *of* it. Suffering the extreme devastation of will and self-control that addiction brings, people necessarily become self-centered. The humiliation, shame, and guilt that erode self-esteem also breed deviousness and manipulation. Severely addicted people feel unworthy and incapable of getting what they need in straightforward ways, no matter what masks of competence or grandiosity they may wear. It is true, then, that a particular kind of personality distortion occurs with addiction, not as its cause but as its effect. It is an addict*ed* personality instead of an addict*ive* personality.[2]

If we cannot blame addiction on some preexisting personality problem, we must look elsewhere for its causes. We will find considerable help in the more modern understandings of behavioral psychology.

Behavioral Insights

The roots of behavioral psychology go back to a seventeenth-century philosophical idea called *associationism*. Beginning in the thinking of the philosophers Berkeley, Hobbes, Locke, and Mills, and later verified in direct experiments by psychologists and physiologists, associationism recognized that new patterns of activity or learning occur because one sensation or response becomes associated with another. The best-known early experimenter in this arena was the Russian physiologist Ivan Pavlov. His studies of conditioned behavior in dogs spawned a whole field of studies of how human beings learn, adapt, and respond to the world around them. Pavlov inaugurated modern behavioral psychology.

In contrast to psychoanalysis, behavioral psychology restricts itself to objectively observable behavior; it avoids considering interior, subjective experience. So not only is behavioral psychology more precise and verifiable than psychoanalytic theory, but it also focuses on dynamics of learning and habit formation, which have been somewhat ignored by psychoanalysis.

In behavioral psychology, *the law of effect* replaces what Freud called the pleasure principle. The law of effect simply says that if a behavior is associated with an effect of pleasure or relief from pain, that behavior tends to occur more frequently. This is a component of learning called *positive reinforcement*. Conversely, if a behavior is associated with pain or removal of pleasure, it will tend to occur less frequently (*negative reinforcement*). Repeated experiences of association between behaviors and their effects constitute the form of learning known as *conditioning*.[3]

Simply stated, if I do something that makes me feel good, I am likely to do it again. If I keep doing it, and if it keeps making me feel good, I will probably make a habit of it. Once I have made a habit of it, it becomes important to me and I will miss it if it is taken away. In other words, I have become attached to it. The most important behavioral insight into addiction, then, is that attachment takes place through a process of *learning*. The learning need not take place on a conscious, intentional level; it is not a matter of consciously noticing the effects of a behavior and then deciding to make a habit of it. Instead, the process takes place automatically at a deep physical level. In fact, most such learnings never do reach conscious awareness until they are already well entrenched, and many may never come into awareness at all. Because habits and attachments formed through this conditioning process are so deep and automatic, they can be extremely powerful and difficult to break.

To spiritually sensitive people, behavioral psychology sometimes seems cold, austere, unresponsive to the subtle feelings of the human heart. It is true that behaviorists try to base their observations on objective, measurable phenomena; they feel, rightly, that science requires precision. But it is precision that makes behavioral observations so helpful in clarifying the development of addictions. If we combine some relatively simple behavioral understandings with a few psychoanalytic insights and with the actual experience of addicted people, we can form a workable—and I think quite accurate—model of how addictions develop through the process of attachment.

How Attachment Happens

We can understand the attachment process as occurring in three stages, which I call *learning, habit formation,* and *struggle* (see Figure 3–1).

Stage One—Learning

The learning stage is characterized by associating a specific behavior with a feeling of pleasure or relief from pain. Let us say I engage in a behavior. It might be any behavior, intentional or unintentional, from taking a drug to counting my money, from biting my nails to thinking of God in a certain way. When

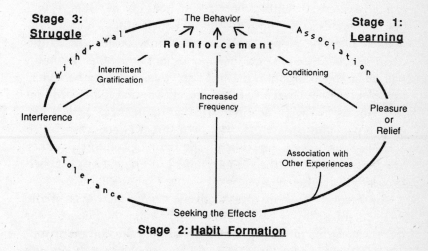

Figure 3–1: The Process of Attachment

I first perform this particular activity, I experience a feeling of pleasure or relief from distress.[4]

My brain automatically *associates* these effects with the behavior. If the pleasurable effect is immediate and powerful, my brain will make a strong association between the behavior and its effect in this single experience, and already it will be pushing to repeat the behavior. If the feelings are weaker or less immediate, it may take many reenactments of the behavior for my brain to solidify the association and start to request repeat performances. Either way, each time the behavior occurs, the association is *reinforced*, making me more likely to repeat it. Thus, certain attachments can develop almost instantaneously, while others may take a long time. This form of learning is known as *conditioning;* it is the primary way we "learn" to be addicted, and it can happen altogether unconsciously.[5]

Stage Two—Habit Formation

Up until now, the behavior and its effects have been associated only with each other. When the conditioned pattern becomes associated with other experiences in my life, I will become more active in repeating the behavior. Then a full-fledged habit develops. For example, I may be feeling a little depressed because of some disappointment in my life. My brain will make the association that if I "do" this particular behavior, I will feel better. Therefore I find myself wanting to perform the behavior as a way of dealing with the depression. Now I not only repeat the behavior for its own direct effects, but I also actively seek it as a reaction to stress or discomfort in other areas of life. This is the primary effect of Stage Two: *increased frequency* of the behavior.

The second stage involves actively *seeking the effects* of the behavior in a variety of life situations. Doing the behavior for its effects seems much more intentional than the automatic repetitions of Stage One, but it can still happen completely outside of consciousness. In most cases, I will be totally unaware that I am using the behavior in this way until Stage Three, when something prevents me from performing the behavior, or when it starts to cause problems.

Stage Three—Struggle

By now my associations have become so entrenched that the habit is an integral part of my life. Upon encountering any upset or distress, my desire to do the behavior surfaces like a reflex. And even in the absence of stress, I begin to feel uneasy if I go too long without repeating the behavior. Whether the behavior involves taking a chemical, losing myself in some pleasurable interpersonal experience, or holding a particular image of God, I am now becoming dependent upon it, needing it, and wanting more and more of it. This is the beginning of *tolerance*.

With this increasing need and frequency, something is bound to *interfere* with my habit sooner or later. Such interferences may occur in any number of ways. If my behavior involves a drug, food, money, or some other substance, I may have trouble keeping myself supplied. If it involves another person, any change in the relationship will threaten my attachment. Or perhaps someone points out my growing dependency, or I become aware of it on my own and decide to quit or moderate it. In this last case, I myself become the source of the interference.

Regardless of how such interferences arise, the behavior that I have become accustomed to is blocked, and I react with distress. In other words, the habit has now become its own source of stress. In addition, the blocking of the behavior produces backlash feelings that are the opposite of those that first caused the conditioning; instead of pleasure, I feel pain. Depending on the nature of the behavior, this distress and pain may range from mild uneasiness to true agony. Either way, the circle of attachment is completed with *withdrawal symptoms*.

For several reasons, interferences actually reinforce rather than lighten my attachment. First, since I have now learned to deal with stress by repeating the behavior, the stress of having my behavior interfered with only makes me want to perform the behavior more. If I become my own source of interference by trying to quit, I learn firsthand about mixed motivations as my attempts to quit continually increase my desire to continue!

Second, behavioral psychologists have long known that *intermittent gratification* is a powerful means of conditioning. A habit is more strongly reinforced when the positive effects of the behavior occur intermittently than when they are constant. This is one reason gambling, fishing, hunting, and other behaviors that have intermittent and unpredictable payoffs are so addictive. It is also why attempts to moderate or cut down an addictive behavior usually fail so abysmally. In my struggles to make gratification less constant, I am actually reinforcing my attachment.[6]

The implications are clear. The only effective way of ending an addictive behavior is to *stop* it. Anything less will almost surely aggravate the situation. But of course I will neither be able to accept nor to accomplish this simple reality. All the pieces of the circle of attachment have reinforced my addictive behavior, making me repeat it. And with each repetition, my learning has become more deeply ingrained. With the circle complete, addiction is born. Even when I consciously try to stop the behavior, my brain is unconsciously learning it better and seeking it more. My motivations are truly mixed, and I am fully at war with myself. My attachment has become like quicksand; the more I struggle and flail about with my willpower, the more mired down I become. All the mind tricks and self-deceptions we have spoken of now come into play—rationalizations and denials and the seductiveness of "I can handle it." My self-esteem crumbles as I sense how truly out of control I am. I am in the clutches of the enemy, and the enemy is clearly myself.

The Development of Aversion Addictions

As I have said, the dynamics of aversion addictions are mirror images of those of attraction addictions. This is portrayed in Figure 3–2.

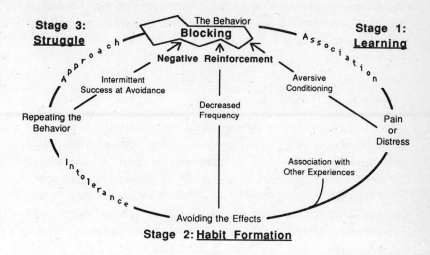

Figure 3–2: The Process of Aversion Attachment

The diagram demonstrates that the power of aversion attachment is invested in *blocking* a specific behavior, avoiding a particular experience. It does this through *negative reinforcement*. An initial association is made between the behavior and unpleasant effects of pain or distress. This is the basis of *aversive conditioning*. Repeated aversive conditionings and associations with other aspects of life cause one to actively avoid the experience and its effects. This leads to *intolerance,* the opposite of tolerance, in which even the smallest taste of the experience is repulsive. A good example would be getting food poisoning from a particular food; for months or years afterwards even the smell of that food can be repugnant.[7]

If the experience cannot be avoided, one undergoes what might be called *approach symptoms,* feelings of repulsion, panic, and anxiety not at all unlike the withdrawal symptoms of attraction attachment. Examples of approach symptoms include the panic experienced by phobics who must fly in a plane, climb to a height, or be confined in a small space, and the repulsion felt by anorexics who are forced to eat. Just as all aspects of attraction addiction serve to perpetuate a behavior, everything here seeks to avoid it.

Summary

I have presented only an outline of the psychological dynamics of addiction. The actual process is more complicated. Human experience can never be captured in charts or diagrams, nor does it ever fit neatly into stages and phases. For example, the effects of a behavior are never wholly pleasurable or painful; there is always a mixture of positive feelings that reinforce the development of an attraction addiction and negative ones that interfere with it. In addition, I have not done justice to the impacts of genetic inheritance, early childhood conditioning, or social and cultural forces, all of which exert powerful determining effects upon the kinds of addictions a given person develops. It has been well demonstrated, for example, that a propensity for alcohol addiction can be genetically inherited. It is reasonable to assume that other such specific proclivities are also a part of our genetic makeup. Our basic humanity means we will be addicted, but our individual heredities have much to say about the specific forms our worst addictions may take.

Finally, the dynamics I have described are based solely on psychological observations and theories; they reveal very little of what is really going on in the brain. In the mid–twentieth century, some authorities began to think of the brain as a "black box." Psychoanalytically, we can listen to a person's subjective account of what is going on in that black box. Behaviorally, we can observe the external results of those mysterious interior happenings. From these accounts and observations, we create theories about what might be actually going on in the box.

Sooner or later, however, we reach a situation in which, as Nobel laureate F. H. C. Crick says, "Several rival theories all explain the observed results equally well. At that point," Crick continues, "there is no choice but to poke inside the box." It remains for neurology to shed light upon the actual workings inside that box, and this is where we must now look.[8]

4. BODY: The Neurological Nature of Addiction

A mind is a system of ideas, each with the excitement it arouses, and with tendencies impulsive and inhibitive, which mutually check or reinforce one another.

WILLIAM JAMES

Most people nowadays are trying to give up the distinctions that used to be made among body, mind, and spirit. Neurological science has effectively demonstrated that mind is brain and brain is body, and many theologians have recovered the old Hebrew sense that humans are beings who *are* souls rather than bodies that *have* souls.[1]

These developments have brought a welcome holism to modern thought. But we should not forget that mind, spirit, and body are not exactly the same thing. Human beings are certainly not made up of compartments, but neither are we conglomerations of undifferentiated mush. If we are to understand ourselves at all, we need precision in how we describe ourselves. Even Eastern religions, which have never compartmentalized human beings as Western society has, establish clear distinctions among different aspects of the human person.[2]

One might assume that Western society, with its great emphasis on science and its long history of compartmentalizations, would be very precise about such things as mind, body, and spirit. But nothing could be further from the truth. Compartmentalizations of the human being have brought us confusion instead of clarity. Richard Restak, a neurologist and widely read author, tells a poignant story about the great neurosurgeon Wilder Penfield's struggle with these distinctions. On a hill near his house, Penfield had painted symbols for spirit and brain on a large rock. He connected the symbols with a solid line. Later, just six months before he died, Penfield climbed the hill again and replaced the solid line with a dotted one. This account, and others recorded by Restak, demonstrate how many neuroscientists can be perplexed by conflicting understandings of mind, spirit, soul, and the like. Much of the time, the problem is language. The old Greek word *psyche* is one of the worst culprits; it has been used for both "mind" and "soul," sometimes for "spirit," and even for the Freudian-Jungian "unconscious." The German *Geist*, meaning both "mind" and "spirit," can be similarly confusing.[3]

To semantic complexity we must add the results of modern neurological research, which make distinctions between mind and body virtually impossible. Most scientists, and many theologians as well, find such confusions intolerable. Out of frustration, one is tempted to jump to the abrupt and arbitrary, as in this statement by French neurologist Jean-Pierre Changeux: "Man no longer has a need for the 'Spirit'; it is enough for him to be Neuronal Man."[4]

Semantic confusions could be helped a great deal by careful research and accurate definition of terms.[5] But the problem goes deeper. Neurologists can be very precise about the brain, and theologians can define terms clearly, but when it comes to the more mystical dimensions of human spirit, those transcending the body and reflecting the divine, theologians as well as neuroscientists face a real struggle. The human spirit, for example, is both pervasively indwelling and yet immutably rooted in the eternal; like God, it has at once qualities of immanence and transcendence. It is our life force as incarnate beings, and yet it is also more. According to Genesis, our human spirit is the breath of God in us. If so, it not only gives us the life we have but also calls us toward a more perfect and whole life, a life of growing freedom and love. Thus the human spirit is the source of our yearning as well as of our very life.

I have not found it easy to bring spiritual understanding into meaningful harmony with the hard data of anatomy and physiology. This is not because of any inherent split between spirit and matter. Instead, the problem comes from my own attitude. I can marvel at the wondrous creation that is the human body. I can try to grasp the fact that the atoms that make it up are almost completely filled with space. I can even appreciate the spiritual nature of the fundamental energy out of which both space and material are made. These are all mysteries to me. The workings of the brain are mysterious in the same way, yet I easily become intoxicated with how much we do know about them. Our knowledge has expanded by quantum leaps in the last few years, and the more I learn of it, the more I am entranced by the possibility of finally knowing everything there is to know about it and thereby being able to master and control it. It reminds me of the serpent's seduction of Adam and Eve: "Eat of the tree of knowledge and you will become like gods."

I find it difficult to walk the line between seeking to expand my knowledge and expecting that knowledge to save me. The truth, of course, is that the farther our knowledge of a thing expands, the more mysterious it becomes. Modern physics has discovered this, and in the process physicists have become less hard and objective; they have become more like artists. The neurosurgeon Wilder Penfield exemplified it as he tried to draw his perceptions of human being on a rock. Ultimately, we cannot grasp everything in its entirety. Yet we would do ourselves and our Creator a great disservice if we did not explore the mysteries of life with every resource available to us. As I describe how the brain functions in addiction, then, I will be as accurate as I possibly can. I shall also use a metaphor now and then, not simply to make a point more clear, but also because I am convinced it will add to the truth of what I am trying to portray.

The Cells of the Brain

Like every other part of the body, the human brain is made of cells. There are many kinds of cells in the brain, but the most significant are nerve cells or *neurons*. Each neuron can be considered a living being in its own right, with its own unique life and experience. Each has its own energies, activities, rhythms of sleep and wakefulness, even its own initiatives. Early in its life, each neuron is capable of movement and reproduction. Each consumes nutrients, breathes oxygen, gives off carbon dioxide and other wastes, and responds to the activities of other cells and to substances in its environment. During its lifetime a neuron is born, matures, learns, ages, and eventually dies. Neurons both initiate and respond to a wide variety of electrical, magnetic, chemical, and vibratory stimuli.

The brain as a whole can be seen as a "colony" in which billions of these tiny cells live. Within this great community of cells, neurons form complex "societies" according to their location and function. The key to any brain activity is the way thousands or millions of these cells interact in *local groups* and *functional systems*.

Local groups of neurons are collections that are located close together in the same areas of the brain (Figure 4–1). Cells in local groups may or may not work together. *Functional systems* are made up of cells that do work together to accomplish certain tasks; they may be located close together or at some distance from one another (Figure 4–2).

Some functional systems are primarily made up of cells within a certain local group. For example, the cells involved in thinking a single abstract thought may be located quite near one another in the frontal lobe. A similar group of cells in the parietal lobe may register a simple touch or temperature sensation. In the same way, a group of cells near the inside center of the brain affects body temperature, and another group nearer the spinal cord is important in governing the level of wakefulness and attentiveness.

But most functional systems involve the collaboration of cells that are widely separated within the brain. Hearing a particular song and having it remind you of a time in the past, for example, involves the cooperation of cells in the inner ear, parietal lobe, frontal lobe, temporal lobe, and a number of other areas as well.

An individual cell is likely to participate in activities with nearby cells in its local group as well as with faraway cells in different functional systems. The *body* of such a cell will be located in a certain geographic area of the brain, but it will send a long fiber or *axon* to another part of the brain to connect with other cells (Fig. 4–2).

Synapses, Neurotransmitters, and Neuroreceptors

In order to work together, nerve cells need to communicate. They send messages through connections called *synapses*. An average neuron has twenty thousand of these connections with other cells; some have as many as two hundred thousand. At each synapse, communication takes place when the axon of one cell releases a chemical called a *neurotransmitter*. This chemical passes across the tiny synaptic cleft between the cells and is

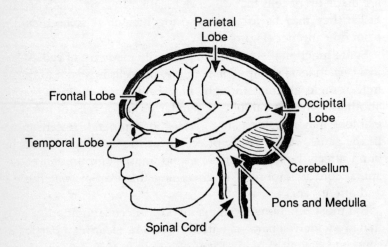

Figure 4–1: Local Groups of Cells

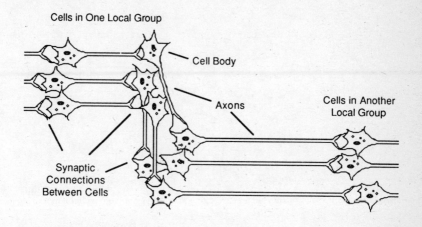

Figure 4–2: A Functional System of Cells

received by a chemical structure called a *neuroreceptor* on the next cell (Fig. 4–3).

In addition to responding to neurotransmitters from other cells at synapses, neuroreceptors are also sensitive to chemicals such as hormones that are produced elsewhere in the body and circulate through the bloodstream. Foreign chemicals such as caffeine, nicotine, narcotics, and other drugs also reach neuroreceptors through the bloodstream and can exert powerful influences on the neurons.[6]

The Complexity of the Brain

No one knows for certain how many neurons exist within the normal human brain; they are literally uncountable. The best

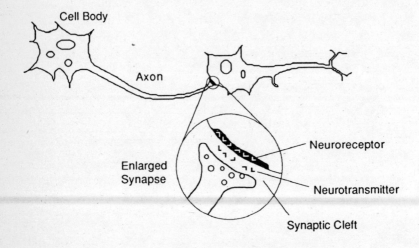

Figure 4–3: A Synapse Between Two Cells

estimates range from ten billion to one trillion. We do know that neurons begin to form early in fetal life, and that by the tenth week of gestation they are multiplying at enormous speeds. Since all the neurons of the brain are formed by the time of birth, they must develop at a rate of at least 150 per second throughout the nine months of pregnancy.

If neurons have an average of twenty thousand synapses each, the total number of synapses in the brain is in the order of five hundred trillion. Such numbers are incomprehensible; if we had a supercomputer that could count a thousand synapses each second, it would take between ten and fifteen thousand years to come to the total for one human brain.

To this magnitude of numbers we must add the incredible complexities of how nerve cells and their synapses actually function. Approximately thirty different neurotransmitter chemicals have been identified thus far, and more will surely be discovered in years to come. Although a given cell normally produces only one kind of neurotransmitter, it is likely to have receptors for a wide variety of transmitter chemicals. Thus a particular cell may be involved in many different functions and will respond to many different stimuli simultaneously.

In addition, communication among cells is not a simple one-way event. Through an important mechanism called *feedback*, cells often respond to the messages they receive by affecting the cells that sent the messages in the first place. Feedback changes the kinds or degrees of messages being communicated and helps maintain the important *balances* we mentioned in the example of congestants and decongestants in Sally's nose.

The messages carried by a specific neurotransmitter may *stimulate, inhibit,* or *facilitate* a cell's activity. The structure of the neuroreceptor on the receiving cell determines which of these effects a certain neurotransmitter will have. Thus one neurotransmitter chemical may stimulate one kind of receiving cell, inhibit another, and facilitate yet a third.[7]

Out of this vast array of interactions, human experience and behavior arise. All thoughts and feelings, all sensations and memories are mediated by the transmission of electrochemical energies along the bodies and fibers of nerve cells and across synapses. The unique patterns of each mental function are determined by which nerve cells and synapses are active, in what sequence, and what neurotransmitter chemicals are released and received. A simple knee-jerk reflex may involve only a few hundred thousand neuron-synapse connections and perhaps only one or two kinds of neurotransmitter chemicals. Complex activities requiring thought, judgment, and action require millions or billions of connections, along with multiple neurotransmitter chemicals in an orchestration so intricate we could never hope to decipher it completely.[8]

All the varying interactions form dynamic systems within systems which mutually affect one another to produce arrays of possibilities approaching infinity. In the light of such magnitude, one can justifiably despair at ever fully comprehending the dynamics of even the simplest mental function, let alone the more complex wonders of creative human experience. Even with the quantum leaps we have taken in the last decade in our understanding of the human brain, and expecting more to come, there are innumerable ways in which we will remain mysteries to ourselves.

Thus anything I can say about how addiction develops in the brain will of necessity be a vast oversimplification—a description of only the most superficial levels of observation. For the rest, as for the stars and galaxies around us, we must experience wonder.

Equilibrium and Stress

As a first step toward appreciating how the brain functions in addiction, we need to review the importance of balance and equilibrium in brain activity. The societies and systems of brain cells form a very real ecology in which equilibrium of activity is critically important. All brain functioning, like the rest of bodily activity, depends upon delicate shifts of balance among chemicals, cells, and systems of cells.

Like human beings, nerve cells can never act in complete isolation from one another. Their interconnections are so extensive that anything happening anywhere within the nervous system is bound to have effects elsewhere. A change in one cell shifts the balance of its local group and of all its functional systems. These changes, in turn, affect the larger systems of the brain, and these then cause changes in the other systems of the body. The great "ecological system" that is the person is altered.

In truth, we must acknowledge that the reverberation of effects is not limited to an individual human being. As we well know, a change in one person affects other people. The individual affects family and friends; these in turn shift the balances of the larger society, and on it goes. Certainly the activities of one nerve cell in the occipital lobe of your brain will not measurably affect the life of someone on the other side of the world, but it cannot be denied that some reverberation, however miniscule, must happen. Just as the billions of cells in each of our brains form a vast interconnected community inside our skulls, so do we human beings—whether we wish to or not—participate in the community that is our earth, our solar system, our galaxy. And just as vast universal systems depend upon their natural ecological balances, so do the systems of cells within our brains.

Both Eastern and Western medical sciences have long understood that maintaining natural balances is the body's greatest priority; if the systems of the body are going to work at all, they must work together in harmony.[9] When equilibrium is thrown off balance, the result is *stress*. By definition, stress is the body's reaction to disequilibrium. Stress includes both the alarm responses that signal imbalance and the coping mechanisms that seek restoration of equilibrium. Within the nervous system, cells cope with imbalances by means of three basic responses: feedback, habituation, and adaptation. These three mechanisms are also the neurological dynamics of attachment. Progressively, like three stair steps descending into slavery, feedback, habituation, and adaptation lead to addiction.

Feedback

I have said that certain results of a cell's activity can be fed back to it by other cells, causing it to modify its functioning. Feedback is the first line of defense against stress, the initial reaction to imbalance. Feedback can occur in one of three ways: cells that are overactive may be inhibited; cells that are underactive may be stimulated; and cells that are doing well may be facilitated.

As an example of inhibitory feedback, let us say I am walking barefoot and I step on a tack. Systems change; stress occurs. Cells in my spinal cord have almost instantly caused a reflex withdrawal of my foot. At the same time, thousands of cells higher up in my spinal cord become very active in response to the sensation of pain. They are sending messages of alarm and stress to functional systems higher up in my brain, demanding response. Unchecked, the alarm messages could imbalance my higher systems, causing me to overreact, to panic, to become crazed over a minor incident. To restore a semblance of equilibrium, and to enable an effective response, some of the receiving cells will send inhibiting messages back to the original cells, in essence telling them to settle down. In this way, the balance of function is kept from being too distorted, and an appropriate response is possible. My higher systems then only have to increase my pulse and respiration temporarily, get me to curse and hop up and down a few times, and help me pull the tack out of my foot.

Although we must remember that millions of cells are involved in any such activity, we can liken feedback between two individual cells to two people talking together. If the first person is speaking at a normal volume and rate and saying something the second person is very interested in, the listener may give facilitating feedback by saying, "Oh, yes, please go on." If the first person is speaking too softly to be heard, the listener will experience a little stress. She may then give some stimulatory feedback: "I can't hear you; please speak up a little." Or if the first person is very excited, speaking too loudly and rapidly, as the nerve cells were in the last example, the listener may feel quite stressed and need to draw back and say, "Whoa, slow down. Now tell me slowly and quietly." This is inhibitory feedback.

The vast majority of feedback that naturally occurs in the brain is inhibitory. The cell systems that initiate activity are, for the most part, in a constant state of readiness and potential activity, so the higher systems of the brain must maintain balance and function primarily by inhibiting them. The cerebral cortex inhibits deeper centers; the right and left sides of the brain mutually inhibit each other; cells in the brainstem inhibit cells in the spinal cord. Effective action primarily takes place through selective inhibition.[10]

I have often marveled at this arrangement of things. It seems to indicate that human beings—and perhaps all other creatures with brains—are inherently active, dynamic, vibrant. Maybe it is in the nature of sentient life not to have to be stimulated in order to act, but to be always ready to go. It means we are not simply passive responders to external stimuli. In the very essence of our being, we are initiators. Perhaps, in the image of our Creator, we ourselves are endless creators.

To return to our earlier analogy, the most common relationship between neurons is like the listening person telling the excited person to settle down and speak more slowly. If this inhibitory feedback works, the excited person calms down quickly, the normal balance of the relationship is restored, and effective communication can continue. If the initial feedback is not effective, however, or if it must be given repeatedly, the listener will experience even more stress. Her next option is more aggressive; she can try to force him to shut up. Failing this, she will try to tune him out. In nerve cells, the two responses happen simultaneously. It is as if the listening person both stuffs cotton in her ears and clamps her hands over the speaking person's mouth. In the language of neurology, habituation has begun.

Habituation

Habituation can be a misleading term; it does *not* mean forming a habit. As we shall see, habituation is the neurological cause of tolerance, but technically it refers only to the process by which nerve cells become less sensitive and responsive to repeated stimuli. Habituation can occur in two ways, depending on how long the stress persists.

The first kind of habituation occurs when cells continue to receive repetitive stimuli over a short period of time, perhaps only minutes or hours. The cells actually restrict the transmission of the incoming impulses by inhibiting their own receptors and by actively suppressing the conduction of those impulses by the sending cells. The receiving cells are no longer simply informing the sending cells of their excessive activity; now they are using brute force to restrict the conduction of impulses along the axons of the sending cells.

We experience such habituation countless times each day. It is what makes us unaware of background noises. When you first go for a walk on an ocean beach, you appreciate the sound of the breaking waves. Since this sound is so repetitive and does not demand any particular response from you, however, you will soon become unaware of it. A long time may go by before you notice it again. This is because the receptors of cells in your auditory system have become less sensitive to that sound, and its conduction along fibers connecting those cells is actively being suppressed. It happens with virtually any system of cells in the brain. When you first enter a building you notice the smells, sounds, and general atmosphere of the place. After a few minutes pass, you usually become unaware of these things.

A number of studies indicate that certain forms of meditation help to decrease automatic habituation, thus enabling one to remain more continually attentive to all that is happening in the present moment. The meditations that work in this way encourage an attitude of relaxed openness, not tense concentration.[11]

We use a similar kind of suppression when we are paying attention to or concentrating on one thing and trying to shut out distractions. It is also a way that psychological repression happens, keeping unwanted internal sensations from entering consciousness. It can take a lot of work to suppress the transmission of internal and external stimuli, especially if the unwanted sensations are strong. This is why we become tired after a long period of concentrated attention, and why active psychological repression can sap our energy for other things.[12]

Because of the effort receiving cells must use to suppress the transmission of unwanted stimuli, they would become exhausted—depleted of neurotransmitters and energy sources—if they kept it up for too long. Therefore a different technique is necessary to handle stimuli that go on for more than a few hours. In this second form of habituation, the nerve cells begin to undergo actual physical changes. They start to destroy their own neuroreceptors and even sever their synaptic connections with the sending cells.[13]

The analogy of two people talking becomes absurd at this point. We would have to say the listening person first punctured her own eardrums and then walked out of the room. So let us drop the analogy for a moment and simply say that full habituation involves actual physical changes in nerve cells and in the connections between them. The physical changes establish a long-lasting system of defense to protect the equilibrium of the larger system. This is the real meaning of habituation.

Both feedback and habituation are ways of trying to keep new stimuli from too strongly affecting the normal equilibrium of ongoing systems. Feedback simply communicates a "quiet down" message. Habituation uses more force to prevent messages from entering the systems it is trying to protect. When neither feedback nor habituation is effective, the repeated messages move in and disturb the natural balance of the systems. Then a new balance must be created. A new normality must be established. This is adaptation. Another word for it is attachment.

Adaptation

If all attempts at habituation have failed, the receiving cells will increase their responsiveness; they will "join in" rather than trying to "tune out." As a result, the normal interaction among cells is thrown out of balance. Once again, the process produces stress.

If this imbalance lasts only a short time, the old equilibrium can be quickly restored when the situation passes. But if the change is prolonged, the rest of the system must adapt to it.

Countless systems of cells must adjust their functioning to accommodate the new situation. When adaptation is complete, stress goes away because a new equilibrium has been established. With this new equilibrium comes a new sense of normality.

A mild example of a change in normality is adjusting to different time zones. If I take a brief trip to the other side of the continent, the time there will feel unusual and a bit stressful to me. I will probably try to hold on to my old sense of time until I return home to my normal time zone. But if I spend more than a few days there, I will have to adapt; if I do not, the stress of trying to hold on to my old rhythms will become too great. When I do adapt, the new time will become normal for me, and my old time zone, when I return, will seem unusual. With each change, I experience stress when my old normality is altered, relief when the new normality is established.

Adaptations occur through physical changes in the cells of the nervous system: synapses formed and dissolved, connections established and broken, neurotransmitters changed in kind and amount, neuroreceptors altered in number and responsiveness. Adapting to change, then, means going through the stress of withdrawal from the old normality and finding relief when a new normality is established. At this most basic level of human functioning, attachment has made its appearance. I am attached to whatever makes things normal for me. I don't let that normality change without a struggle.

We human beings are the most adaptable creatures in God's creation. Our adaptability has allowed us to dominate the world. But our very capacity to create new normalities for ourselves also makes us vulnerable to countless attachments. As every attachment forms, a new normality is born. With each new normality, addiction exists.

Nerve Cells and Attachment

With some understanding of feedback, habituation, and adaptation, we can proceed to examine how attachment actually

happens to brain cells, how the brain becomes addicted. In a
hypothetical example, we will focus on a single synapse between two individual cells (Figure 4–4). It is important to remember that this focus on one synapse and two cells is a vast
oversimplification at the outset; the events I will portray are
actually determined by hundreds of thousands of cells and millions of synapses, including so many variables that the full sequence could never be fully described.

Let us say that the synapse in Figure 4–4 is located deep in
your medulla, just above your spinal cord. It is part of a functional system that helps govern your level of alertness and
wakefulness. The body of cell A is located in your frontal lobe,
and it sends its axon a distance of about six inches down to
your medulla where it forms the synapse with cell B. Cell A's
primary function is to stimulate cell B whenever you need more
alertness. To do this, cell A releases neurotransmitter chemicals

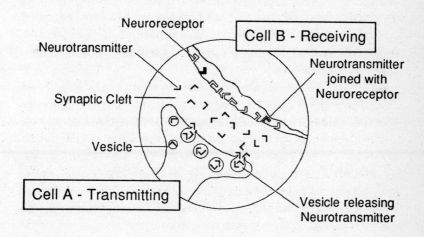

Figure 4–4: Enlarged Synapse

that it has manufactured in its vesicles. Some neurotransmitters cross the synaptic cleft to join with cell B's neuroreceptors, stimulating cell B to send its own messages along to other cells. Soon you wake up and pay more attention to things. When it is time to sleep, cell A quiets down and transmits less, and cell B, receiving less, also settles down. All the changes are kept within a balance and rhythm to which all the cells in this great system have become accustomed; it is "normal."

Then suppose that one day you become upset over something, perhaps an unexpected bill or a threatened relationship. Your general level of agitation rises higher than normal. Cell A sends more signals all day long, and it keeps on sending them after bedtime. You have trouble getting to sleep. While dutifully relaying wake-up signals, cell B also sends inhibitory feedback to cell A, trying to get it to slow down. Sooner or later the feedback will combine with fatigue, and cell A will get the message. If you have relaxed as much as possible and allowed this process to take place naturally, sleep will come. A normal equilibrium will have been reestablished. At the turn of the century, before people knew much about how nerve cells worked, professor Edwin Starbuck understood the natural balances of the brain. "Let one do all in one's power," he said, "and one's nervous system will do the rest."[14]

But let us say you choose to handle your insomnia in a more unnatural way, by taking a sleeping pill. The sedative interferes with cell A's ability to send its neurotransmitter chemical to cell B. Cell B, noticing a less than normal amount of chemical, sends stimulatory feedback, trying to get cell A to become more active. Cell A may answer weakly by releasing a little more neurotransmitter, but the sedative prevents it from fully responding. The sedative has overwhelmed the normal process, feedback has not helped, and sleep comes.

If you take sleeping pills only one or two nights, your cells can usually reestablish their normal balance of functioning without much difficulty. The first night or two without the sedative may be more restless as the cells readjust, but things are then likely to return to normal quite quickly. If you continue to take the pills, however, you will surely become addicted.

When the sedatives first appeared on the scene, they immediately forced cell A to quiet down. But if their presence continues for more than a day or two, cell A begins to habituate to them. By changing its own physical structures, it becomes less sensitive and responsive to the sedative's effects. Soon you notice that the original amount of sedative no longer works. You have to take more in order to get to sleep. In this way habituation causes *tolerance*.

If you continue to take the increasing amounts that are necessary to get to sleep, you keep overwhelming cell A's habituation. You have effectively stifled its capacity to manufacture and send its neurotransmitter to cell B. Neither cell A's habituation nor cell B's stimulatory feedback has been able to preserve the interior balance. The effects of the sedative have proceeded well into your alertness system, and the whole system must adapt.

Cell B adapts by changing its neuroreceptors. When cell A was releasing a normal amount of neurotransmitter, cell B had just the right number and kind of neuroreceptors to receive exactly the amount needed to get its job done. But now the sedatives have caused cell A to release far less neurotransmitter. After its stimulatory feedback fails, cell B builds more receptors, as if hoping to catch as many stray molecules of neurotransmitter as possible. It also increases the sensitivity of these receptors, to get the greatest stimulation possible from the few transmitters available.

By adapting, cell B establishes a different balance within the system, a new normality. While cell A continues to function at a low level, cell B now has many more receptors that are much more sensitive, and it is therefore able to send along its own messages to other cells with a fairly adequate level of strength and frequency. Things are not back to normal, but the new normality feels good enough. Until you stop taking the pills.

Let's assume that you decide to quit the pills; your stress is over and you think you can get back to normal on your own. Or perhaps you run out of pills and cannot get a refill. Either way, the sedatives disappear from your brain. Cell A, now completely accustomed to large amounts of the sedative, quite literally goes crazy when it experiences none at all. It *rebounds* by firing up to an extreme degree, manufacturing and releasing great quantities of the wake-up neurotransmitter. The neurotransmitter molecules come raging in hordes across the synapse, invading cell B's receptors, which, as we have said, are now much greater in number and much more sensitive. The effect on cell B is cataclysmic. Its messages to other cells are berserk, unintelligible. All the millions of other neurons that had so dutifully adapted to their new normality are now screaming that something is terribly wrong, and you are experiencing both the backlash and the stress that constitute withdrawal symptoms.

Your agitation increases dramatically. Stress signals are sent into body control centers deep in the center of your brain; your heart beats faster, your temperature rises, your muscles tighten and twitch, your thoughts race. Countless other systems of cells that have also become accustomed to the presence of the sedative start reacting to the stress. In your frontal and temporal lobes, cell systems that have associated the sedatives with relaxation now start yelling for a fix. It is as if they were shouting, "Take some more! Take some more!" while other frontotemporal systems counter with, "You shouldn't—you'll become addicted!" But of course the addiction has already happened.

The battle of the will has begun. Different functional systems that used to be balanced are now contradicting one another, producing mixed motivations. Some of them are trying to stop, and others are fighting desperately to keep the addiction going. All the functional systems that constitute your capacity for self-deception are brought into play. At some point the "I can handle it" systems fire up. We know the rest of the story.[15]

Chemicals like sedatives can be very addictive because they affect the brain directly. Some substances even have chemical components identical to the body's own natural neurotransmitter chemicals. Such substances are extremely addictive because receptors for their chemicals already exist on cells in the brain. For example, the body creates natural pain-relieving neurotransmitter chemicals called *endorphins* and *enkephalins*. Receptor sites for these chemicals occur naturally on many cells in the brain and elsewhere in the body. When a substance like morphine that has the same kind of chemical structure is taken into the body, it joins with these receptors immediately, and its effects are extreme. Similar natural receptors exist for certain stimulants and tranquilizers. Chemicals like morphine and amphetamines, which create sensations of pleasure and relief from pain along with directly affecting natural neuroreceptors, are the most addictive of all known substances.[16]

Nonsubstance Addictions

I have used chemical substances in this explanation of addiction because their effects are so rapid and powerful. But the same kind of cellular dynamics apply to nonsubstance addictions. If we had been talking about addiction to money, power, or relationships, even if we had been talking about addiction to images of ourselves or of God, we could have said much the same about what happens to our nerve cells. We would probably be speaking of different systems of cells, but the patterns of feedback, habituation, and adaptation would be essentially the same.

As an example, consider a very minor addiction, one that seems to harbor no special destructiveness. Let us say that I have established a morning routine of having a cup of coffee and reading the paper before starting the day. I enjoy the quiet, undemanding quality of this time and would be loathe to call it an addiction. But I have been engaging in this little routine for years, and the cells of my brain have become adapted to it. They are used to the whole sequence of the time: the gentle slowness of waking up, the familiarity of my favorite chair, the gradual stimulation of the reading, the friendly jolt of the coffee's caffeine playing out its own little addiction fix, the sounds of the house waking up around me. All the countless sensations and behaviors of this time have become mutually associated in patterned sequences of synapses, with billions of cells having become adapted to certain amounts of neurotransmitters in certain ways at certain times. It is normal.

Then a couple of days come along in which something interferes with this routine. Perhaps I had to stay up later than usual the night before, so I sleep longer and have to get up in a rush, drinking my coffee on the way out the door and missing the paper entirely. Although I may not even think about it consciously at the time, my body and mind feel as if something is not right. I'm more irritable and grouchy than usual. I may even find myself a little shaky and out of sorts for the rest of the day. It all happens because the cells of my brain have not received what they have learned to accept as normal doses of neurotransmitters in normal sequences and rhythms, and they are reacting with stress. They feel something is wrong.

My irritability and shakiness are mild withdrawal symptoms from a minor addiction. Although the withdrawal symptoms in this example are far less severe than those of chemical addiction, vast numbers of cell systems are involved. Apparently "minor" addictions often influence so many other systems that they wind up involving more cells than some chemical addictions do.[17]

Therefore, a person who becomes temporarily addicted to narcotic painkillers in the hospital may be able to withdraw from the drug more quickly and with much greater serenity than another person can withdraw from the loss of a job or a loved one. The first person's addiction, although chemically intense, involves perhaps only a few million cells directly. It has not had time to influence such larger systems of cells as those having to do with the meaning of life, self-image, and basic security. In the case of losing a job or a loved one, great existential systems are deeply affected by withdrawal, even though the direct impact on any given synapse may not be so great. Thus the brief chemical addiction can be seen as a temporary and primarily physical discomfort, but the nonsubstance addiction digs deeply into the ground of the person's sense of meaning and selfhood.

Multisystem Involvement

In prolonged addictions, what may initially have involved a rather simple change in a few million synapses has progressively expanded to affect billions of cells in countless other functional systems. One after another, each system has tried to defend against the initial imbalance, failed, and adapted by establishing a new normality. In turn, it causes an imbalance in the next system, and on the process goes. It is not so difficult to understand how our addictions can come to rule our lives. Each of our major addictions consists not only of the primary attachment itself; it also includes the involvement of multiple other systems that have been affected by it. To put it quite simply, addictions are never single problems. As soon as we try to break a real addiction, we discover that in many respects it has become a way of life.[18]

Because of multisystem involvement, breaking an addiction usually requires changes in many different areas of life. A person trying to stop smoking will find the struggle much greater after eating, after sex, or at other times that have become associated with cigarettes. An alcoholic is likely to fall off the wagon if she frequents the same old bar, as is a narcotic addict who continues to associate with the same old friends. A person who is trying to be less attached to money will find it much more difficult if he continues his habit of listening to the stock market reports several times a day. The workaholic won't be helped by continuing to spend all her social time with other workaholics, nor will the overeater gain anything but weight by continuing to gaze into the refrigerator whenever he has a spare moment. Similarly, a person who wants to spend more time in prayer and less in doing things is unlikely to gain much if she uses her prayer time to think about the things she should be doing.

Multisystem involvement is also responsible for temporary experiences of freedom when a person's environment changes. A compulsive overeater, for example, will struggle in agony with his addiction to food while in his usual environment. But if he goes on a backpacking trip in the mountains, he may feel quite free of the addiction. In the new environment, he is sufficiently removed from other stimuli that have become associated with his addiction, and he can much more easily deal with his primary urge to eat. He may even think he has finally overcome the problem, only to be deeply disappointed when he returns to his usual surroundings and finds all of his associations triggered afresh. Similarly, a narcotic addict may feel no great desire for drugs when she is hospitalized or in prison, only to reexperience the full power of her addiction upon return to "real life."[19]

The longer an addiction continues, the more things will become associated with it and the more entrenched it will become. Some behaviors or chemicals that produce a rapid, direct, and powerful effect may result in addiction after only one or two experiences. Others may require many repeated experiences before they become entrenched. But regardless of how an addiction begins, the longer it lasts the more powerful it becomes. Attachments are thus like spreading malignancies, steadily invading and incorporating their surroundings into themselves. To apply the words of Isaiah, addictions are like "greedy dogs, never satisfied," or as Habakkuk said, "Forever on the move, with an appetite as large as sheol, and as insatiable as death."[20]

Stress Addiction

The phenomenon of becoming attached to stress itself is of particular spiritual significance, and it is a good example of multiple system involvement. Only recently described, stress addiction has received considerable attention in the popular press. Therefore I will discuss it only briefly in the context of neurology.

The body naturally creates adrenaline, noradrenaline, and other chemicals that are important in responding to stressful situations. In addition, some of the body's natural opiates, such as the endorphins and enkephalins, are often released in times of stress. All these stress chemicals act as neurotransmitters. They may be generated by nerve cells and act as message carriers across synapses, or they may be released elsewhere in the body and travel through the bloodstream as hormones. Adrenaline, for example, is manufactured by the adrenal gland and acts as a hormone. Whether stress chemicals come across synapses or through the bloodstream, they exert powerful effects when they arrive at neuroreceptors of nerve cells.

Normally, the body is accustomed to a low level of stress chemicals in the circulation, with intermittent bursts of higher amounts during times of crisis. Most normal stresses are of relatively short duration, and the brain's natural responses cope with them quickly. In our hectic modern society, however, many individuals find themselves in prolonged stressful situations. Many jobs today are geared to continually high stress levels, and some professionals even pride themselves on the amount of stress they habitually live with. The effects of such protracted stress have been well demonstrated in terms of heart disease, ulcers, and the like. Jogging and other exercise programs, by stressing the body physically, help accustom the body to coping with high stress levels so it more readily handles them as normal. With all of this, stress becomes a habit.

What happens is not difficult to understand. In responding naturally to a stressful situation, the body increases its production of stress chemicals. The chemicals have their expected effects on the cells that receive them, and things return to normal when the stress passes. But if the stress continues, the receiving cells must cope. They try their feedback mechanisms to achieve a lower level of stress chemicals, and, if this doesn't work, they habituate and adapt. Their adaptations establish a new normality that includes an excessive quantity of stress chemicals.

The body suffers in a variety of ways. The circulatory system, for example, must adjust to a normality that includes much more work. Of special significance to our discussion, however, is what happens when the stress-addicted person tries to relax and slow down. If the person takes a vacation, goes on a retreat, or even tries to settle down to pray for a while, the removal of external stress causes less stress chemicals to be generated. This is precisely what the person wants and expects—a time of relaxation—but she does not expect the response of her brain cells to this reduction of stress chemicals. The neurons, having adapted to high levels of stress chemicals, now react as if something were wrong. They send signals, ironically, of stress to the rest of the body, trying to get things going again. Thus the person who is trying to settle down may find herself becoming increasingly anxious, looking around for something to do, and not at all experiencing the rest and relaxation she had hoped for.

Further, other cells that have become habituated to stress chemicals may go through a backlash withdrawal and "crash"; they become lethargic in what now seems to them a virtual absence of stimulation. Thus in addition to agitation, the person may also feel great fatigue and sleepiness. "I never knew how tired I really was until I settled down." Again, both phenomena tend to encourage the person not to relax. The choice is limited: either a crashlike sleep (which is often impossible because of agitation) or just getting back to doing something demanding and stressful. A severely stress-addicted person can thus be in a completely no win situation, becoming increasingly fatigued but at the same time increasingly uncomfortable with any situation that might offer rest.

In most average cases of stress addiction, people simply find they need extra time to wind down before they can begin to relax. Some individuals know this pattern so well that they plan their vacations around it. "I have to take at least a two-week vacation because it takes me almost a week to relax, then a few days just to sleep, and then I can have a couple of really enjoyable days." With more severe stress addiction, people may be totally unable to relax unless they do something that gives them their fix of stress chemicals. Many people choose jogging or some other physically stressing activity. Such activities have become immensely popular among the stress-addicted because they provide enough chemicals to keep withdrawal symptoms at bay, while at the same time freeing the mind from normal worries and work tasks.

It is in the realm of spiritual practice, however, that attachment to stress becomes most obvious. Spending time in quiet, receptive openness is an essential part of prayer, meditation, and most other spiritual practices. In such settings, even mild addiction to stress becomes rapidly and painfully evident. For many modern spiritual pilgrims, the simple matter of taking time for daily prayer can become a battle of will excruciatingly reminiscent of that encountered in chemical addiction. The mind can generate wondrous excuses to do something instead of just being open and present. The struggles that go on between being and doing can be awesome. Issues of control and willpower, surrender and defeat rage with all the drama of true spiritual warfare.

There are many things all of us might rather avoid in prayer: we might rather not relinquish our sense of self-mastery; we might rather not hear what God might ask of us; we might rather avoid the self-knowledge that comes to us in quiet. Now, in addition, increasing numbers of us are discovering that we would rather not experience the discomfort of being peaceful.

Permanence

As we have seen, the process of attachment takes place psychologically as a form of learning. This learning happens through reinforcement and conditioning, and it is accompanied by physical and chemical changes in the brain and elsewhere in the body. Since multiple functional systems are involved, the learning becomes entrenched.

Sadly, the brain never completely forgets what it has learned. Because of the deep and pervasive physical power of strong attachments, their potential exists forever in us, even after we have effectively broken the habit of acting upon them. We may joke about never forgetting how to ride a bicycle, saying, "Don't worry; it will come back to you." But the permanence of addiction memory is not funny. It stands ready to come back to us with only the slightest encouragement. The brain learns how to "do" its attachments far better than it learns to ride a bicycle or drive a car, and it remembers them more powerfully. Years after a major addiction has been conquered, the smallest association, the tiniest taste, can fire up old cellular patterns once again.

One aspect of addiction, then, is permanent. Thus we never completely overcome our attachments. Because staying away from addictive behavior is an ongoing business, people in AA call themselves "recovering alcoholics" rather than "recovered alcoholics." We may control our behavior in response to our addictions, and we may, with grace, be delivered from bondage to them. Then, as time passes, their pull becomes less intense. But throughout our lives, their potential for reactivation continues to exist within us. The brain does not forget. From the standpoint of psychology, this means we can never become so well adjusted that we can stop being vigilant. From a neurological viewpoint, it means the cells of our best-intentioned systems can never eradicate the countless other systems that have been addicted. And from a spiritual perspective, it means that no matter how much grace God has blessed us with, we forever remain dependent upon its continuing flow.

5. SPIRIT: The Theological Nature of Addiction

I stood there, hugging my mattress, and smiled with happiness. . . .
"Are you from freedom?" they asked me.

ALEKSANDR SOLZHENITSYN

We all come "from freedom" originally, and we are meant *for* freedom. But addiction holds us back from our rightful destiny; it makes us prisoners of our own impulses and slaves to our own selfish idols. This is our condition, and the Scriptures of the great world religions attest to it.

God creates each one of us uniquely, and, as the psalmist affirms, our creation is good: "It was you who created my inmost self, and put me together in my mother's womb. . . . I thank you for the wonder of myself, for the wonder of your works." God creates us out of love and loves our goodness: "I have called you by name and you are mine. . . . You are precious in my eyes, and honored, and I love you." God lovingly creates us for a life of fullness and freedom: "I know the plans I have in mind for you . . . plans for peace, not disaster, reserving a future full of hope for you." Finally, God creates us *for* love; the call of our creation is for us to love God, one another, and ourselves: "You shall have no gods except me"; "You shall love God with all your heart, with all your soul, with all your strength"; "You must love your neighbor as yourself."[1]

And yet, as the Eden account so clearly testifies, our creation also includes temptation and attachment. Because of this, our love of God, neighbor, and self is not pure and whole, and we are not free enough to follow God's call with our own power. We must struggle, and we stand in need of grace. Such Scriptures describe the threefold nature of the human spiritual condition: God creates us for love and freedom, attachment hinders us, and grace is necessary for salvation. In and throughout this condition, God loves and longs for us, and we love and long for God.

Displacement of Spiritual Longing

I began this book with the statement that all human beings have an inborn desire for God. In Thomas Merton's words, "There is a natural desire for heaven, for the fruition of God, in us."[2]

Ultimately, our yearning for God is the most important aspect of our humanity, our most precious treasure; it gives our existence meaning and direction. There has been considerable debate about whether this "human religious impulse" really is universal, whether it represents a true primary drive, and so on. I am convinced that it is indeed universal and primary, and, moreover, that it is a very specific desire for an actual loving communion, even union, in an absolutely personal relationship with God.[3]

I think it is this desire that Paul spoke of when he tried to explain the unknown God to the Athenians: "It is God who gives to all people life and breath and all things. . . . *God created us to seek God*, with the hope that we might grope after God through the shadows of our ignorance, and find God." The psalms are full of expressions of deep longing for God: thirsting, hungering, yearning. And God promises a response: "When you seek me with all your heart, I will let you find me."[4]

For me, the energy of our basic desire for God *is* the human spirit, planted within us and nourished endlessly by the Holy Spirit of God. In this light, the spiritual significance of addiction is not just that we lose freedom through attachment to things, nor even that things so easily become our ultimate concerns. Of much more importance is that we try to *fulfill our longing for God* through objects of attachment. For example, God wants to be our perfect lover, but instead we seek perfection in human relationships and are disappointed when our lovers cannot love us perfectly. God wants to provide our ultimate security, but we seek our safety in power and possessions and then find we must continually worry about them. We seek satisfaction of our spiritual longing in a host of ways that may have very little to do with God. And, sooner or later, we are disappointed.

From a psychoanalytic perspective, one could say we *displace* our longing for God upon other things; we cathect them instead of God. Behaviorally, we are conditioned to seek objects by the positive and negative reinforcements of our own private experience and by the messages of parents, peers, and culture. Even the briefest look at television and magazine advertising reveals how strongly our culture reinforces attachment to things other than God, and what high value it gives to willful self-determination and mastery. Mediating all the stimuli they receive, the cells of our brains are continually seeking equilibrium, developing patterns of adaptation that constitute what is normal. Thus the more we become accustomed to seeking spiritual satisfaction through things other than God, the more abnormal and stressful it becomes to look for God directly.

From a more specifically spiritual viewpoint, we naturally seek the least threatening ways of trying to satisfy our longing for God, ways that protect our sense of personal power and require the least sacrifice. Even when we *know* that our hunger is for God alone, we will still be looking for loopholes—ways of having our cake and eating it too, ways of maintaining our attachments to things and people while simultaneously trying to deepen our intimacy with God. We seek compromise not because we are evil or conniving, but because of the way we are made; we naturally look for the least painful ways of living. From the standpoint of basic human common sense, this is perfectly reasonable. We look for our ultimate satisfaction in God's palpable and definable creations instead of looking through them to the hidden, loving face of their Creator.

Perhaps our displacement of desire for God makes sense from God's perspective as well. After all, it is God who creates us with our propensities for addiction. In fact, it seems to me that

God actually encourages such displacements. I shall discuss this more theologically at the end of this chapter, but let me explain some of it now. Most of the time, God remains somewhat hidden from us. Why? For one thing, God in immanence is already too close to us, too intimate, too much at one with us to be a clear-cut object, and God in transcendence is too great to be apprehended.[5]

More importantly, however, I think Paul's words about the unknown God indicate another reason for God's hiddenness; full and freely chosen love for God requires searching and groping. What would happen to our freedom if God, our perfect lover, were to appear before us with such objective clarity that all our doubts disappeared? We would experience a kind of love, to be sure, but it would be love like a reflex. Almost without thought, we would fix all our desires upon this Divine Object, try to grasp and possess it, addict ourselves to it. I think God refuses to be an object for attachment because God desires full love, not addiction. Love born of true freedom, love free from attachment, requires that we search for a deepening awareness of God, just as God freely reaches out to us.

In addition, full love for God means we must turn to God *over and against* other things. If our choice of God is to be made with integrity, we must first have felt other attractions and chosen, painfully, not to make them our gods. True love, then, is not only born of freedom; it is also born of difficult choice. A mature and meaningful love must say something like, "I have experienced other goodnesses, and they are beautiful, but it is You, my true heart's desire, whom I choose above all." We have to turn away before we can come home with dignity.

Homecoming

For many of us, freedom of choice means that our longing for the true God remains submerged within us for months, years, or even decades at a time, while our conscious energies seek satisfaction elsewhere. The true longing will resurface periodically, giving us small gracious and discomforting nudges, as if to say, "You know this is not *really* what you want." But the momentum of attachment usually carries us on, with a power all its own. Often it is not until this momentum brings us to some point of existential despair, some rock bottom, some *impasse*, that we become capable of beginning to reclaim our true desire.[6]

Sometimes we hit the impasse during what has been called midlife crisis; more often despair seems to be given through grace in times and circumstances that are completely unpredictable. Whenever and however it happens, we look at the attachments that had seemed so important and feel like the idol maker in Isaiah: "What I have in my hand is nothing but a lie!" And we hear, more clearly than ever, God's call to "make your home in me, as I make mine in you."[7]

With this realization, we may begin to reclaim our primary desire for God. Like the prodigal, we may choose to come home. But at this point, after years of displacing desire and of adapting to addictions elsewhere, home will not seem normal. Thus we respond to God's homeward call with a mixture of hope and fear. Something in us knows that this home is where we belong, but in many ways it also feels like alien territory. The journey homeward, the process of homemaking in God, involves withdrawal from addictive behaviors that have become normal for us. In withdrawal, attachments are lessened, and their energy is freed for simpler, purer desire and care. In other words, human desire is freed for love. Constance FitzGerald puts it this way: "In the process of affective redemption, desire is not suppressed or destroyed, but gradually transferred, purified, transformed, set on fire. We go *through* the struggles and ambiguities of human desire to integration and personal wholeness."[8]

There are many spiritual names for this homecoming process: detachment, affective redemption, purification, purgation, ongoing conversion, sanctification. The term FitzGerald uses, *transformation of desire*, is the most appealing. As I said earlier in discussing detachment, this process is easily misunderstood no matter what we call it. To appreciate it with accuracy, we need to acknowledge both its beauty and its fierceness. It is beautiful because it is a homecoming, because it is a liberation from slavery, and because it enables love. But it is fierce because it entails relinquishment, letting go, risking, and enduring losses that are very real and very painful.

What we lose in homecoming is not the objects of our attachment, nor even our care for them. In fact, our care grows toward true love, love that sees and appreciates all things in the world for what they are. What we lose is the attachment itself, the strength of our addictive behavior in relationship to these objects, the way we make gods of them. But we feel no real consolation when we experience the inevitable withdrawal symptoms that accompany letting go our attachments. There is real pain here. If I am a heroin addict in withdrawal, I will not be consoled by knowing that heroin will still exist in the world after I withdraw from it. What I want, and what I am losing, is the *use* of it. Similarly, if I am withdrawing from addiction to a relationship or possession, it will not ease my sense of loss to know that the person or thing will continue to be present in my life or in my heart. I will not even want to hear that my love will be stronger if I let it go. What I cling to most is my *use*, my idolization of that person or thing.

The loss of attachment is the loss of something very real; it is physical. We will resist this loss as long as we possibly can. When withdrawal does happen, it will hurt. And, after it is over, we will mourn. Only then, when we have completed the grieving over our lost attachment, will we breathe the fresh air of freedom with appreciation and gratitude.

When we first reclaim our spiritual longing, we usually do not know that the journey homeward will involve such relinquishment, that the homemaking process will be so painful. Perhaps this is just as well. Not that such knowledge would cause us to choose against God; on the contrary, I think the greater danger is that those who think they understand the process are likely to try to make it happen on their own by engaging in false austerities and love-denying self-deprivations. They will not wait for God's timing; they will rush ahead of grace. I have seen it happen when ascetic practices have become overinstitutionalized, and I have engaged in it myself when I thought I could engineer my own salvation. It does not work. Once we begin to experience the authentic homeward process, however, the implications of withdrawal become increasingly clear. If we allow grace to guide our responses, we will realize what we need to know as we need to know it.

One of the most powerful and potentially frightening realizations is that there is no new normality of freedom to replace the old ones of addiction. As I have said, there can be no addiction to the true God because God refuses to be an object. God is more with us, more intimate, more steady than anything else in life. God is our ever-present Creator, Sustainer, and Redeemer. God is the one completely passionate and faithful Lover of our lives. And yet, God is never "normal."

Massive implications follow for the conduct of the spiritual life. I, for one, would very much like to have a prescribed method of living that would insure my relationship with God and keep my spiritual growth on track. Although I would probably rebel against some aspects of such a system, I would at least feel certain of its limits and demands. I could adapt to it, make it my normality, and feel secure within it. But addiction to a religious system, like addiction to anything else, brings slavery, not freedom. The structures of religion are meant to mediate God's self-revelation through community; they are not meant to be substitute gods. Doctrines of belief, rules of life, standards of conduct, and reliance on Scripture are all essential aspects of an authentic spiritual life. Sacraments are special means of grace; God acts through them with great power. All these things are vehicles for God's love, but addiction to them makes them obstacles to the freedom of our own hearts.

It is impossible to "adapt" to God or to true freedom and love. We can—and, temporarily, we will—make images of God, freedom, and love and try to form them into new normalities that we can cling to, but these attachments must eventually be lifted as well. Authentic freedom and love will not be captured by attachment. Therefore, the journey homeward does not lead toward new, more sophisticated addictions. If it is truly homeward, it leads toward liberation from addiction altogether. Obviously, it is a lifelong process.

Self-Image

Let us examine one way the homeward journey might appear from the inside, from the standpoint of interior spiritual experience. We must begin with our sense of self. When we were infants, we had a very different sense of self than we do now as adults. Then, before we had words, images, or concepts that we could label as "me," we had a simple sense of being, a diffuse, undifferentiated awareness in which nothing separated us from what we perceived. When we reexperience that quality of awareness, as we all sometimes do, we might call it *unitive*.

But throughout our life since infancy, our brain cells have been developing countless patterns and sequences that more clearly separate, define, and secure our sense of self. Brain cell patterns involve functional systems throughout all parts of the brain: memory, thought, body senses, visual images, everything. Thus our self-images, whatever we feel is "me" at a given time, are in fact cellular representations of self.

By the time we become adults, we have hundreds, perhaps thousands, of these self-representation systems. Some of them function when we experience ourselves at work, others when we are at play, still others as parents, spouses, and all the other roles and circumstances within which we may pause to notice. Beneath the variety of self-representation systems, we sense something more constant, a vague awareness of "me-ness." This constancy allows us to feel we are ourselves no matter what particular role we may be playing at a given time.

For the most part, however, we pay no attention to the underlying constancy. Instead, we act on the basis of our varied self-representation systems, changing from one to another in accord with our roles and situations. If we are fairly well adjusted psychologically, our different systems will be generally harmonious and easily interchangeable; we can shift flexibly from one to another. If not, we may have to expend considerable energy to keep them from warring with one another.

If we look at the makeup of our self-representation systems, it is obvious that they are intimately associated with our addictions. The strongest components of any self-representation, the ones that are most important, are the adaptations other systems have made to that particular role. When I sense myself as a writer, for example, my self-representation is associated not only with simple memories and hopes of writing, but more strongly with my attachments to writing: the ego issues of being considered an authority, the desires and fears associated with success and failure, competitiveness, and the like. Attachments come to the forefront of my self-consciousness because, whether I like them or not, they have entrenched themselves as significant. I want to see myself as a writer who is simply living out a few of God's gifts gracefully. But what I really see is my attachments.

I could say similar things about my images of myself as father, as husband, as man, as spiritual pilgrim and lover of God, or any other self-representational system. We all define ourselves according to our addictions. If I were to ask you to tell me about yourself, and you replied honestly, you would tell me about your attachments. And if you weren't honest, even *that* would be because of your attachments.

Ideally, our self-representation systems should function as expedient tools for us. They help us understand our own unique personalities; they differentiate us from one another; they let us know where our own character stops and where someone else's begins. These self-discriminations are necessary for us to live efficiently, and they can also help us appreciate the wonder of our own being. But not only are our self-representation systems strongly determined by addiction; they also become objects of attachment themselves. Some self-images we want to cling to; others we abhor. As in any other addiction, when we become addicted to our own self-images, they begin to control us.

For example, I am seduced and enticed by a certain image of myself as a whole, holy, loving man who is well on his way to becoming free from attachments. When this image comes up in my prayer, it causes me to pose and posture; I find myself trying to make my prayer fit my image of how a holy man would pray. I no longer really invite God into my prayer. It becomes an act, a scene I play out on my own stage for my own edification. God is there in spite of this silliness, but, for the time being, I am unaware of that saving fact.

So we become addicted to our own self-images. Our cellular representations of self habituate, adapt, and control us. In the course of homecoming, addictions to self-image also must be lightened; they must be relinquished in the cause of freedom. As I understand it, this is the neurological meaning of "losing oneself to find oneself" and "dying to be reborn." As with other addictions, we do not readily relinquish our attachments to self-images. In fact, we may cling to them more tenaciously than to any other attachments. Although the process of relinquishment is really only a matter of easing the power that certain cell systems have over our sense of self, it can indeed feel like death.

If we examine our experience with self-representations, however, we may find reassurance in the fact that we already, and very naturally, experience their coming and going, their death and rebirth, countless times each day. We have so many self-representations, and they are almost constantly changing. They dance around in accord with our circumstances; first one comes to prominence in our awareness, then another, then still another. Viewed from this perspective, it is difficult to believe how desperately we try to cling to them.

Even more surprising and reassuring is the frequency with which our self-representations disappear from awareness entirely. In the brain, their disappearances are characterized by pauses in the normally hectic firing of self-defining systems, as if the cells all just happened to take a breath and rest for a while. Our interior experience at such times is one of self-forgetfulness or self-transcendence. For a moment, we are relieved of bondage to who we think we are, and we can simply be. Usually these moments are very brief, because the systems of our brain start to experience withdrawal and quickly reestablish their normal conditioned patterns.

Thus, although pauses in self-definition may happen thousands of times a day, they happen so quickly that most of them go unnoticed. Occasionally, however, they are prolonged. At these times, we appreciate their spaciousness and freedom. We experience wonder and awe and a kind of sacred remembrance of what our awareness was like when we were very young. These times of just being remind us of home. We call them "spiritual" or "unitive."[9]

The Experience of Heart

Such pauses in self-definition are like moments when a cloudy sky breaks clear. If only for an instant, we catch a glimpse of the spaciousness that always exists behind the clouds. There, in that pure and indefinable blueness, we get a sense of what the sky is really like. Similarly, when the clouds of our self-images clear for a moment, we catch glimpses of something that is constant behind our ever-changing representations of self. This underlying constancy of self does not change with our different roles, nor does it seem to be influenced by any particular characteristics. It also seems amazingly elusive, disappearing just as we try to grasp it, hiding when we seek it, appearing again when we least expect it.

We find ourselves becoming a bit anxious if we try to look too closely at our interior constancy, precisely because it is so indefinable. We are apt to want to call it our true self, the "real me." But to call it "me" never seems quite right, for it fits into none of our other systems of self-representation. It permits of no particular neurological associations, except perhaps with some memory, similarly vague and indefinable, of "home." We cannot hook it to this or that; we cannot give it an adequate name; we cannot control it. We can avoid awareness of it, but it never bows to our will. Therefore, though it haunts us beautifully and calls us sweetly, we do fear it.

If we are given the grace to spend some time with this mysterious constancy, just gently letting it be what it is, we may find a strange confidence, even security, growing out of it. Here is something solid, some foundation of self that is invulnerable to any other experience, unaffected by anything else that might happen to us. It has something to do with just being aware and alive, for we notice it when we notice our own attention. In fact, we notice it most precisely when our attention has been temporarily captured by an attachment and then returns to some central position of pure awareness. In the return we feel a sense of security; for whenever our attention goes away and then returns, the presence at the center is still there, unaffected, unchanged, and somehow free.

As nearly as I can tell, our core is what Hebrew and Christian spiritualities have called *heart*. It is the aspect of oneself that is not only one's own center but also where one can be in closest, most directly feeling contact with the presence of God. And it is meant to be the center of our will, the nucleus of all choice and action. Further, it is where we realize our essential unity with one another, with all God's creation. Yet this heart sense does not want to be pinned down even with contemplative concepts. The heart does not seem to be quite oneself nor quite God. In the same way that it refuses to associate with any of our conditioned images of self, it does not fit any of our images of God. Thus it remains continually frustrating, and we always find ourselves deeply unknowing in the face of it.[10]

The problem is that this heart sense is so *spacious*. It seems to have no bounds, no qualities, no form. It is unconditioned and unconditional. It has no objective attributes that we can grasp and relate to other systems. Since we can neither make an adequate cellular representation of it nor incorporate it into our preexisting systems, we cannot adapt to it. Like God, and perhaps in the image of God, our deepest sense of self will never be "normal." Because our brains are used to dealing with normalities that have boundaries and qualities, the spaciousness, its beckoning security and confidence notwithstanding, is terrifying.

So we are likely to pull away, perhaps even with vengeance, and thrust our attention back into the world of form and substance where we can define ourselves. Here, though our addictions bind and frustrate us, we at least think we know who we are. We are in the world of our normality, the conditioned world to which the cells of our brain have adapted. But we have been touched by this other, deeper sense, and it will touch us again. It has awakened and appetized our spiritual hunger, and part of us will forever want to go back for more. We can occupy ourselves with other things, but there will always be times of rest, moments of pause, and there it will be, beckoning.

Spiritual Growth

Given enough experiences of pauses in self-definition, we may come up with a partial solution. During the experiences themselves, this heart sense is completely ungraspable. But afterward we do have a memory of the experience, and with this memory we can make an image, a representation. We can give the image a name, just as I have done in this discussion. We can say it is heart, center, true self, experience of closeness to God. We can then associate this cellular representation with our previous images of God and self and begin to build a framework of spiritual understanding around it. Our representation, of course, will never be the thing itself, but it does help us reflect upon it, communicate about it, and otherwise dance about its edges.

If we are halfway authentic in our searching, we must take time in silence—in prayer and meditation. Like other normal human spiritual pilgrims, we will spend most prayer time playing with our spiritual images and representations. But within the spaces created by our attempts to be quiet, there will always be moments when we find ourselves opening once again into the *reality.* Then we will be reminded, if grace gives us the courage to admit it, that we have been chasing images instead of truth, perhaps even worshiping our representations as if they were idols. After each such reminder, we will come away with yet another memory representation, perhaps more sophisticated than those that went before. By now we may have learned to make such images readily; we may even have made a habit of it. We know there is some deception and distancing in this, but we are simply more comfortable dealing with our images than directly facing the awesome, uncontrollable reality those images represent.

As time goes on, and with grace, the representations we make of spiritual reality will become less and less solid. Their qualities and boundaries will become more vague. As this happens, we will discover that we can exist without clinging to our images so desperately. Our clutching, grasping hands begin to relax. From the standpoint of neurology, relaxing means a greater *flexibility* of sequences and patterns among cell systems. We have less need to immediately associate all our experiences with preset representations, to make them fit. We are a little more willing to be unknowing and to be surprised. Slightly more often, more of the cells of our brains may simply register a sensation rather than so quickly having to habituate and adapt to it. Psychologically, we are becoming a little more willing to let things be what they are. Spiritually, we are becoming a little less attached. Freedom is happening.

There is a strange sadness in this growing freedom. Our souls may have been scarred by the chains with which our addictions have bound us, but at least they were familiar chains. We were used to them. And as they loosen, we are likely to feel a vague sense of loss. The things to which we were addicted may still be with us, but we no longer give them the ultimate importance we once did. We are like caged animals beginning to experience freedom, and there is something we miss about the cage.

Like the Israelites in the exodus, we know we do not want to go back to imprisonment, and we sense we are moving on to a better existence, but still we must mourn the loss of the life we had known. This is a poignant grief, yet somehow soft and gentle. With time, it will grow into compassion: compassion for the spiritual imprisonment of our sisters and brothers, and compassion for the many parts of ourselves that still remain in the chains of addiction. Grief and compassion are part of spiritual growth, the homeward pilgrimage from imprisonment to freedom, the homemaking of deepening love.

It is important to note that the spiritual growth process involves far more relinquishment than acquisition. In our culture, we are conditioned to expect growth to involve acquisition of new facts and understandings. To put it neurologically, the functional systems of our brains are used to elaborating upon themselves as growth happens. We have, in a way, become attached to the very process of expanding our attachments. But spiritual growth is different. It cannot be packaged, programmed, or taught. Although some new facts and representations may help us along the way (such as the ones I share in this book, I hope), the essential process is one of transformation, not education. It is, if anything, an unlearning process in which our old ways are cleansed, liberated, and redeemed. As I have indicated repeatedly, spiritual growth does not establish new normalities through more habituation and adaptation. Instead, it frees us from slavery to conditioning; it leads us in the direction of unconditioned love.

Obviously, we cannot "conduct" spiritual growth. At bottom, it is God's work. It is grace. But neither is it something we can be quietistic about. The immanence of God involves us of necessity, and the transcendence of God calls forth a response from our free will. In brief, I think our participation is threefold. First, we pray. Our prayer may be formal words or a simple, silent turning toward God, but it acknowledges our source of hope, expresses our true desire, unites us with the rest of humanity, and commits our willingness to God. Second, insofar as we can, we attend to the heart sense within us; we try to keep returning to it in whatever ways are possible and staying with it as long as we can rather than immediately retreating into our conditioned systems. Third, we try to live the spiritual reality as best we can. This means taking risks of faith, trying to trust the incomprehensibly loving presence of God whether we feel it or not, and being as loving of ourselves and others as we possibly can.

Our threefold participation of prayer, meditation, and action responds to God's graceful initiatives in our lives, and it leads toward a deepening trust in God. Developing fitfully, gradually, and often painfully, this fundamental trust in God allows us to become a little less bound to our addictions. Our security then becomes less dependent on the power of our own brain patterns and more dependent on the unexplainable mercy of God. Finally, as trust grows, we become less self-preoccupied, more free to be attentive to the needs of others, truly more loving.

Spiritual growth is by no means a steady process. Each time we touch the mystery of what is most real, we flee back into "normality" with some deeper layer of attachment threatened. Often upon return we may experience a backlash, a rebound of self-centeredness and desperate attempts to control things. We may find prayer more difficult at such times, and we are almost certain to invent new representations to take the place of those we have had to relinquish. The choices we make on such occa-

sions become very important. Although they do not by themselves determine any outcomes, they do create the patterns of
our freedom and slavery, and these, interwoven with God's patterns of grace, form our unique tapestries of spiritual growth.

Three Responses

The choices that are open to us in response to our experiences of God's loving, threatening call may sometimes be excruciatingly difficult to execute, but they are quite simple to
understand. There are really only three options; we have already touched on them all in our discussion, and most of us
have already used them all extensively in our lives. First, we
may try to deny or avoid God's call, repressing our desire and
displacing its energy. Much of the time we are successful at
this, but the call is bound to break through our defenses and
haunt us with gentle nudges or hound us with relentless yearnings. Second, we may make images of spiritual reality, cellular
representations that enable us to feel a measure of power over
it instead of remaining dependent upon it. Third, we can try to
be present to the mystery in a gentle, open-handed, and coop-
erative way. This is the *contemplative* option—not any system of
complicated exercises, but the simple and courageous attempt
to bear as much as one can of reality just as it is. To be contemplative, then, is not to be a special kind of person. Contemplation is simply trying to face life in a truly undefended and open-
eyed way.[11]

I am convinced that all people are continually involved in
choosing among these three options. Like most other decisions
we make in daily life, our responses to God's call often take
place automatically, without any real reflection. They just happen as results of barely conscious processes that we seldom
take responsibility for. When we do begin to claim our choices
in response to our hunger for God, we have begun an intentional spiritual life. Then, of course, we are liable to go over-
board in the opposite direction, taking it too much upon

ourselves, thinking that the choices we make will absolutely determine our spiritual destiny.

But it is not so simple. Each of the three options has its assets and liabilities, its grace and its dark side. While denial and avoidance are usually only attempts to escape further into the delusion of salvation through attachment, they may, on a temporary and expedient basis, provide us with time and energy to secure ourselves in other areas of life and thereby build up enough courage to turn around and face reality. The making of representations of God can be used to create an artificial puppet god whom we can manipulate superstitiously, but it can also be a way of communicating symbolically with and about the reality of God. And in spite of how reverently I have described the contemplative way, it too can become distorted into denial of life or escapism by devaluing the cellular representations that our brains require to function naturally.[12]

Thus here again we see the gentle uncertainties that always caress our capacity to choose. From the outside of things, there is no way to be sure what the one "right" choice might be at any given time, for grace can be present in "wrong" choices as well. From the inside, where we might be more in touch with our true longing for God, the "right" choice is simply the one that springs most directly from that longing and reflects it most authentically. Prayer, Scripture, sacraments, spiritual community, and self-examination can all be sources of guidance as we seek to make such choices. But finally, even here at the heart of our human freedom, we are dependent upon the mercy of God.

In addition to struggling to make the best choices, we also have the problem of trying to follow through on the choices we make. Because we are addicted, our motivations are always mixed and our hearts are never completely pure. It can therefore be only a part of the self that makes a good choice and cooperates with it; much of the rest of the self is bound to fight it. One set of systems in the brain may choose the way of freedom and love, but countless others will immediately react with stress and mental treachery and all the other ways we have seen of trying to preserve our old normalities. Then, of course, it is all too likely we will start to rely on willpower, resolutions, and "I can handle it."

It all seems very difficult and entrenched. God creates us with our vulnerabilities, our propensities for addiction and willfulness. And then as we grow through life we are tempted and seduced away from our deepest desire, forced to struggle with ourselves, thrust repeatedly back upon our own weakness. One wonders why. I do not know for certain, of course, but I have some thoughts. For me, they come out as the perfect expression of love.

Scripture

"Why?" is a theological question. It means we have to try to look at things from God's standpoint. This is, of course, an ultimately impossible task. But we can do our best, and we are not without resources; we have God's self-revelation through Scripture and human history. The traditions of world religions diverge here, with differences so obvious that their similarities become remarkable. Hindu and Buddhist traditions base the why on *karma* and dependent origination.[13] In contrast, the monotheistic religions trace the ultimate why to God's creative action. Because it is my faith, I will pursue the question from a Christian perspective, grounded in its Jewish roots, and will begin with a review of addiction in Scripture.

Let us return once again to the Eden story in the second and third chapters of Genesis. Temptation, the possibility of attachment, is there at the outset. "God caused to spring from the soil every kind of tree, *enticing to look at and good to eat*, with the tree of life and the tree of the knowledge of good and evil in the middle of the garden."

Freedom of human choice is also complete at the beginning, as evidenced by God's admonition: "You may eat of all the trees in the garden, except for the tree of the knowledge of good and evil, for on the day you eat of it you shall most surely die."

God does not forcibly prevent Eve and Adam from taking the fruit but simply commands them not to. For a while, it seems, they have no reason to turn against God. There is no report of them struggling to stay away from the tree. The threat of God's admonition is sufficient to counteract the enticing nature of the tree. Their motivations are still pure.

Then another force enters. The serpent turns temptation into attachment first by claiming that God was not telling the truth: "No! You will not die!" It then goes on with its own enticement, encouraging the humans to deny their dependency on God and to try to be masters of their own destinies. It tells Eve, in essence, that she can *handle* it: "God knows that on the day you eat it your eyes will be opened and you will be like gods." It was after hearing these words that Eve became truly tempted. Only then did she see "that the tree was good to eat, pleasing to the eye, and desirable for the knowledge that it could give."

The tree is attractive, not simply because of its outward appearance, but also because it offers the possibility of becoming godlike. Who would not be tempted? Yet *becoming godlike* here means distorting one's God-given will into an autonomous willfulness that is antagonistic to God. This is the fundamental and most critical distinction between simple human desire and truly corrosive attachment. The wanting, yearning, longing quality of pure desire is natural and God-given. It is not only necessary for life; it also lends a rich open-endedness to existence, a lack of complete satisfaction that is powerfully creative and, in many ways, joyful. But the grasping, clinging, possessive quality of attachment is something very different. It is restrictive, not creative, imperative instead of enjoyable. As William Blake said, rather than binding ourselves to joy, we must kiss it as it flies.[14]

When God confronts Adam and Eve in their disobedience, they immediately go into mind tricks, excuses, and rationalizations: "The man replied, 'It was the woman you put with me; she gave me the fruit . . .' The woman replied, 'The serpent tempted me . . .'" Their words may sound like simple fast-talking, but, as I have said, I see them with more empathy. To me

they are not really trying to con God. They are honestly confused in their motivations, caught with their fig leaves, and
ashamed. They knew they were responsible for their behavior,
but they also knew something had interfered with their intentions. Such is the nature of attachment, pitting one part of oneself against another. Is the feeling not familiar? I remember
feeling that way as a child: confused, ashamed, guilty, yet wanting to say, "But . . ." In fact, I remember feeling somewhat that
way yesterday. Perhaps we should not condemn Adam and Eve
when, in the face of God, they begin to manifest some of the
qualities of the addicted personality.

In response to the humans' behavior, God says, "I will mul-
tiply your pains in childbearing. . . . With suffering shall you
get your food. . . ." God's response is usually understood as a
straightforward punishment, and it certainly reads that way.
But along the lines of Buddhism's Noble Truths, God's words
are also a statement of the way things are: suffering is a fact of
life, and it is caused by attachment. God then sends them forth
and sets cherubs and a flaming sword "to guard the way to the
tree of life."

Throughout the Genesis account, God may appear afraid that
humans will "reach out and pick also from the tree of life," thus
gaining sufficient divine qualities to become competitors for
God's power and reign. If this were indeed God's motivation, it
would come from attachment to power and glory, and the actions springing from it would be unjust. The cherubs and flaming sword, and the banishment itself, would serve to protect
God against humans. Yet, when read with an appreciation of
human addiction, Genesis becomes the story of a free and purely loving Creator who knows that Eve and Adam will not be
able to withstand the compulsion to eat from that second tree.

Banishment is thus more protection than punishment. The
cherubs and the flaming sword are there to protect humanity's
freedom rather than to defend God's power. In a tender maternal moment before Eve and Adam leave, God makes clothing
for them. This is not the action of a frightened God who clings

to divinity, but of a free and loving God who knows that human life cannot be full unless it depends on its Creator for divinity.

In the Old Testament stories that follow, the Law, Torah, is established to help guide and protect humanity from the inevitable consequences of excessive attachment and its empty promises of autonomy. As the preacher of Ecclesiastes relates, "I denied my eyes nothing that they desired, refused my heart no pleasure. . . . What futility it all was, what chasing after the wind." To state it more positively, the law is a way of grace, established to help foster and mark the path to freedom and love. "Turn me from the path of delusion," the psalmist prays, "grant me the grace of your Law. . . . Had your Law not been my delight I should have perished in my suffering."[15]

There can be no doubt that God is adamant about being God, and there are sure consequences when one denies it. But God's insistence is grounded in love rather than in selfishness. We have had God's breath in us since the beginning, and God knows that the fulfillment we long for will come from nothing other than God's very self. Nothing less than God will satisfy the yearning that God has planted within us.

Thus the powerful, monolithic Yahweh of the Old Testament speaks tenderly and with hope: "Then when you call to me, and come to plead with me, I will listen to you. When you seek me you shall find me, when you seek me with all your heart; I will let you find me. . . ." "Do not be afraid, for I have redeemed you; . . . Should you pass through the sea, I will be with you; or through rivers, they will not swallow you up. Should you walk through fire, the flames will not burn you. For I am your God, the Holy One of Israel, your savior."[16]

When Jesus appeared on earth, his self-proclaimed reason was to fulfill the Torah. He did not wish to change the Law itself, but he vehemently attacked those who were addicted to its letter instead of really loving its author. In the context of addiction, the essence of Jesus' teachings can be seen as threefold. First, he gave a powerful, unequivocal restatement of the necessity of relinquishing attachments in order to love God and neighbor with a full, unfettered heart. "No one can serve two masters. . . . You cannot love both God and money." "Anyone who prefers father or mother . . . son or daughter to me is not worthy of me." Second, he both explained and exemplified the nature of a life free from attachments, lived in true liberation and love. "I am gentle and humble of heart, and you shall find rest for your souls. My yoke is easy, and my burden is light." Third, he established the way toward fulfillment, the Good News.[17]

Jesus' existence as the divine incarnation proved that instead of hoarding the qualities of divinity, God wished to share them through a right relationship with humanity. The events of Jesus' life, leading to his crucifixion, demonstrated the threat he posed to peoples' addictions and the lengths to which they would go to protect their attachments. In turn, the crucifixion itself demonstrated the extent to which God would go to liberate people from their attachments. Jesus proclaimed that there was no greater love than to lay down one's life for one's friends, and then he proceeded to do just that. Finally, and most important of all to the Christian faith, Christ's resurrection proclaimed absolute and unquestioned victory over attachment itself, over its consequences, and over its causes.

Jesus' words about attachment are far too numerous to quote here. They are, however, absolutely relentless and unequivocal. They begin with the two greatest commandments and proceed to the call to love one's neighbor even unto death; to relinquish possessions, occupation, and even family in order to follow God; to take no thought of the morrow, to have no worries about food, clothing, or even what one is to say or do; to become like little children, to lose oneself in order to find one's true self; to die in order to be reborn. Jesus addressed addiction in every conceivable aspect of life, including aversion addictions: prejudices, phobias, and the like. He picked a despised Samaritan as the hero of his story about the love of neighbor; he continually affronted the sensitivities of his peers by trafficking with the most abhorred people; he attacked fear as evidencing lack of faith and went so far as to advocate loving one's enemies.

The Beatitudes of Jesus' Sermon on the Mount are an unparalleled testimony to the glory of freedom from attachment. The blessedness they promise comes not just from heroic battles with one's addictions, but from being unwillingly deprived of their gratification. The poor, the grief-stricken, and the persecuted, for example, have had no choice; they suffer and they need human help, yet, in a way, they may be closer to freedom because they have less to be attached to. Thus Jesus' words not only issue a call to relinquish attachments; they also point out that we cannot do it alone. Liberation finally must come through grace, not solely through one's own efforts. Jesus taught people to pray for grace: "Lead us not into temptation and deliver us from evil, for *thine* is the power. . . ."

Sin, then, is not just ignorance or moral straying, but a kind of bondage or slavery from which one must be delivered into freedom. Freedom is possible through a mysterious, incarnational synthesis of human intention and divine grace. The issue is not simply whether one follows personal attachments or follows God. It is instead a question of aligning one's intention with the God within and with us, through love and in grace. To make the alignment possible, Jesus proclaimed a message of radical forgiveness, not only forgiveness of humanity by God, but also forgiveness of one another by people. In this radical forgiveness, it is even possible to be freed of attachment to one's own guilt for or justification of the wounds one has inflicted upon others. True love of self, a reverence for the essential goodness of God's creation, is made possible. Herein lies the potential for endless freedom in the service of love. Nothing, not even one's own sinfulness, has to remain as an obstacle to the two great commandments.

For Christ, the way to abundant grace and forgiveness is through himself, away from all possible objects of attachment. "I am the way"; "Follow me"; "I am the bread of life"; "I will give you the living water"; "Whoever comes to me will never hunger"; "Come unto me all you who labor. . . ." Jesus was the New Adam, the profound love gift of God entering the world to effect a reconciliation of humanity with God, to restore a right relationship to those who were unfree, who had aligned themselves away from God, who had been crippled in their love. He came for the sinners who had missed the mark of responding to God's love. To put it bluntly, God became incarnate to save the addicted, and that includes all of us.

Addiction and Evil

In the first chapter of this book I called addiction the absolute enemy of human freedom, and in many other places I have used words like *imprisonment, slavery,* and *deliverance* in order to describe actual human experiences of addiction. It is no accident that these words are also used extensively in Scripture to describe subjugation to evil. I have also related addiction to sin. And where I have said Christ is victorious over addiction, traditional Christianity would say Christ is victorious over Satan. It is now time to examine the relationship between addiction and evil. It is not a pleasant topic, and its conclusions are like fire.[18]

To explore how evil relates to the human experience of addiction, we must look at the concept of *temptation*. The Bible includes a wide variety of interpretations of temptation. In much of the New Testament, it is seen as the primary activity of the devil, a seduction. At other times, temptation is viewed as an evil force in and of itself. Elsewhere, it is simply viewed as part of the human condition. Finally, in the Letter of James, it is even seen as something to be grateful for. Some of these writings reflect the Old Testament idea that temptation comes from God as a test, while others, notably James, refute this idea strongly.[19]

In spite of the variety of views as to the source and purpose of temptation, biblical sources show a clear consistency as to its nature: it is the *starting point* of addiction. Whether we see it simply as our biological capacity to become attached, or as a seduction by dark external forces, or both, temptation is always the first step, the preliminary opportunity, for addiction. Once attachment is fully entrenched, our motivations become so mixed that freedom to choose is seriously compromised. But in the stage of temptation, where only the potential for attachment exists, our yes or no can make all the difference.

The biblical words for temptation, *māsāh* in Hebrew and *peir-asmos* in Greek, are also variously translated as "trial," "proving," and "test." Whether *test* means examination or exercise, most modern people are not at all attracted to the notion of being tested by God. Neither am I, and neither, apparently, was the author of the Letter of James. The letter says, "When you have been tempted, never say 'God sent the temptation.'" The whole idea of testing brings back the concept of a fearful, self-protective, and now even ignorant God who must put us to the test to find out whether we are faithful.[20]

But let us look a little more deeply. If we are truly meant to have a free capacity to choose for or against God, if that is really the perfection of God's creative love for us, then the choices we make must be responses to invitations, not to coercions, manipulations, or orders. God, in love, protects our freedom by calling to us, not demanding of us. God's invitations may be dramatic and strong, or still and small, but anything more than invitation will not protect our freedom and potential for love. God will not be a puppet master over humanity.

Moreover, as I have said, God remains somewhat hidden in our lives, not only because of intimate immanence and awesome transcendence, but also because of a loving refusal to become another object of attachment. It would not be freedom to stand face to face with certainty before the God of creation and say yes to "Follow me." Who would say no? Further, this "Follow me" is only a natural consequence of God's more primary request, "Love me." How could true, flowing love be born unless we freely choose the Lover, just as the Lover has first chosen us?

I have also said that truly free choices for love must be made over and against something else. There is no authentic freedom if we are consistently drawn to one clearly preferable option; again, who would choose otherwise? The excruciating reality is that truly free, loving choices cannot be easy. In fact, one might timorously propose that the most free and loving choices are those that call forth the relinquishing of what one holds most dear. It is another meaning of the cross. The joy and beauty of freedom and love *must* be bought with pain. We might wish that God had created things otherwise, so that an easier life could be possible, but a careful look at our own history will prove such a wish empty. It is precisely where we have chosen, most painfully and with greatest personal risk, to say yes to love and freedom that we have found the most richness and joy. Indeed, it is not easy, but we would grow to hate it if it were.

Thus, ironically, we must have attachments if we are to be free. We have to turn away before we can come home with dignity. Just as God invites us toward love, we must be pulled away. Just as we crave freedom, we must be seduced into slavery. It is here, perhaps, that temptation begins to make a little sense in the light of love. It is still not an attractive concept; I do not think it was ever meant to be. Our temptations are trials, certainly. And each of our addictions proves how we have responded—not simply from our conscious will, but from the totality of our being. In a sense, then, temptations are trials and tests of who we are as complete human beings. But they are trials and tests for our own growth, not for God to find out how good we are. God knows that we are good; it is for us to discover that goodness. As we have seen, the tests of attachment, by bringing us to our knees in humility, may show us the way of goodness and allow us to choose that goodness with our whole being.

We might jump to the conclusion that evil, by providing us with temptation and attachment, is really working as God's agent. But it is not so simple. Christian tradition holds no doubt that evil actually and vehemently means to work against, not for, God. Evil is irrevocably at cross-purposes with love, life, freedom, and creation. According to the same tradition, Satan was created free in God's love just as was humanity, and in all of creation Satan most willfully and maliciously chose against God. But the tradition further maintains that Satan has been vanquished; the power of evil is invincibly restrained by grace. Evil continues to work against God, but with no chance of ultimate success. Moreover, there is no power and no condition that God's grace cannot penetrate with love. God can indeed, then, work through the power of evil. Perhaps this is what happens in the phenomenal deliverances that sometimes occur in the most severe addictions, and even more frequently in the many opportunities attachment provides for authentic surrender to God. Grace shines radiantly through addiction.

Finally, in both Old Testament and New, temptation is frequently addressed in the context of God's care and protection. The trials and temptations come, but grace is with us in them, capable of pouring love's vibrant energy through them. Deuteronomy recalls the trials of the wilderness:

God humbled you, and made you feel hunger. God also fed you with food that neither you nor your ancestors had ever known, to make you understand that human beings live not on bread alone but on every word that comes from the mouth of God. The clothes on your back did not wear out and your feet were not swollen, all those forty years.[21]

Grace is much more than a static possibility of love. It is an outpouring, a boundless burning offering of God's self to us, suffering with us, overflowing with tenderness. Grace is God's passion. The New Testament closes with these words:

The Spirit and the Bride say, "Come!"
Let everyone who listens answer, "Come!"
Then let all who are thirsty come:
All who want it may have the water of life,
and have it free.[22]

6. GRACE: The Qualities of Mercy

Life was in the Word, life that was the light of humanity. The light shone in the darkness, and the darkness could not overcome it. We saw its glory, endlessly overflowing with love and grace.

THE GOSPEL ACCORDING TO JOHN

In the arid lands that were the birthplace of monotheistic religion, the desert was a primary symbol of trial and temptation. And water, especially freshly flowing "living" water, became a prominent image of God's grace. Just as fresh water could transform wastelands into gardens, the living water of God's Spirit could cause love to grow within the most parched and willful souls. In the psalms, the soul thirsts for God "as a deer yearns for running waters," "like a dry and weary land." And in Isaiah, God promises grace: "Let the desert rejoice. . . . For waters shall break forth in the thirsty ground. . . . The wasteland will be turned into an Eden. . . . You will become like a watered garden."[1]

Eden, as a garden, becomes symbolic of humanity's rightful relationship with God's grace. It represents both our birthplace and our destiny, our home and our promised land, where we rely upon grace as our ultimate security. Addiction's empty and idolatrous wasteland is transformed by grace into a garden of freedom and love.

I speak of grace with some fear and uncertainty; of all the things I have written about, I can do least justice to this. All I can do is share some of my images, my own "cellular representations" of the mystery that is grace. I hope that my images will touch some of your own and perhaps help them become simpler rather than more complicated, more flexible rather than more frozen.

Images of Grace

Grace is the active expression of God's love. God's love is the root of grace; grace itself is the dynamic flowering of this love; and the good things that result in life are the fruit of this divine process. Grace appears in many ways, which theologians have long attempted to categorize. I do not know the details of these categories, but it is clear that they speak of a love so abundant, so selfless, so endlessly overflowing as to surpass description. Jesus spoke of God as being our intimate, loving parent, and he wished for us to receive God's love like little children. Let me try to use that image, at least for a while.[2]

It is very difficult to understand a mother's love; she loves her baby, finally, just because he is her baby. God's love for us may be something like this. We are God's children, so we are simply loved. Ideally, an infant does not earn her parents' love; they love the baby first. Because of this preexisting love, the parents care for their child. God "graces" us in similar ways. There is grace in the simple gift of our existence, in the opportunity to live consciously and appreciatively in this world, and in the goodness of our nature. There is grace in the natural steadiness of life, in the simple things God gives us. God spontaneously gives us beauty and breath and touches of love, just as parents give their children food and warmth naturally, almost automatically. And there is grace in the steady self-giving of God that protects our freedom and keeps us yearning.[3]

There are also flowerings of grace that seem more eventful and surprising, as when children find unexpected presents for no special reason or receive extra hugs at times of failure and frustration. God attends to us in this way too, surprising us with undeserved, unexpected goodnesses and empowering us when all seems lost. There is also grace in the rougher side of things, as in weaning, or when parents allow their children to struggle toward identity without constantly being taken care of. In a similar way, God lets us make our own decisions, even at times when we would much prefer to be taken care of. God blesses us with responsibility and the dignity it contains.

And there is a particular dimension of grace that is interactive, in which God and person respond mutually to each other's love. Responsive grace is somewhat like a child desiring to please her mother, and the mother responding with special tenderness. The mother responds not to the child's actual behavior, but to the simple love that prompted the behavior. This is one of the most tender flowerings of love. A little boy tries to help his father with some household work, or makes his mother a gift. The help may be nothing more than getting in the way, and the gift may be totally useless, but the love behind it is simple and pure, and the loving response it evokes is virtually uncontrollable. I am sure it is this way between God and us. At the deepest, simplest levels, we just want each other to be happy, to be pleased. Our sincere desire counts far more than any specific success or failure. Thus when we try to pray and cannot, or when we fail in a sincere attempt to be compassionate, God touches us tenderly in return.

Many times, of course, children try to please their parents in a manipulative way. As the father of four, I have learned to become suspicious when one of my offspring mows the lawn or washes the dishes without being asked. I must admit, however, that I do the same thing with God sometimes. I find myself posing and posturing before my images of God, trying to make something happen. But on other occasions the desire to please is simple and pure. It springs not from any desire for gain, but from that deep root where love exists simply for the sake of love. The child's desire to please is a wholly natural and spontaneous expression of love, and it prompts a natural loving response in the other, with no notion of earning, deserving, or achieving.

Beyond this point, the parent-child metaphor becomes a little weak. Human parents can indeed be manipulated, and their loving responses can be earned and achieved. But in God's intimacy every desire is known, every thought and intention perceived before it even takes place. There can be no secrecy between the soul and God, and therefore there can be no manipulation. Although God as our transcendent Creator is indeed a kind of parent, God is far more intimate with us than human parents ever could be, even closer than a pregnant woman is to her unborn child. God's love pervades us, flows through every molecule, vibrates every particle of our being.

The parent-child metaphor also is inadequate when we consider the control parents exert upon their children, especially through punishment and restriction. To some extent, human parents control their children's behavior as a means of protecting and training. God does not act in precisely this way. Although the Old Testament includes many references to God's punishment of humankind, and the New Testament in no way belittles the reality of judgment, God's activity with persons is not *controlling*. Without exception, God preserves and protects our precious edge of human freedom. Without this imperative for final love and freedom, God explains, "The spirit would give way before me, the very souls I have made."[4] Thus God calls us, invites us, and even commands us, but God does not control our response. We alone bear responsibility for the choices we make.

Further, God's love is more constant than human love can be. Human loving has its pure moments, and parental love especially can sometimes express a likeness of God in its deep steadiness. But however solid it may be, human love is always prey to selfishness and distractions bred by attachment. Even in the best of situations, human love is bound to become intermingled with attachment. When this happens, we can feel possessive of our loved ones or jealous or even vengeful if they do not meet our expectations. We can see our loved ones as extensions of ourselves, wanting them to make good impressions on other people so we ourselves will look good. We can want them to live out our fantasies, conform to our desires, meet our needs, provide us with our security and sense of worth. The degree to which we can feel or express authentic love is always conditional upon such attachments.

It is not so with God's love. God goes on loving us regardless of who we are or what we do. This does not mean God is like a permissive human parent who makes excuses and ignores the consequences of a child's behavior. Such permissiveness is more cowardly than loving, because it devalues the child's capacity for dignity and responsibility. In God's constantly respectful love, the consequences of our actions are very real, and they can be horrible, and we *are* responsible. We are even responsible for the compulsive behaviors of our addictions. The freedom that God preserves in us has a double edge. On the one hand, it means God's love and empowerment are always with us. On the other, it means there is no authentic escape from the truth of our own choices.

But even when our choices are destructive and their consequences hurtful, God's love remains unwavering. Thus, regardless of our own insulation and defensiveness, God is constantly open and vulnerable to us. God is joyful when we are joyful and when we bring joy to others. God hurts when we are hurting and when we hurt others. Such is the constancy of God's love. God's Spirit is the vibrant essence of creation and transformation, and grace flowers in constantly surprising ways, but in the root of love that bears this Spirit and grace, God is changeless.[5]

Often, of course, we do not sense the constancy of grace-giving love. In many situations God may seem unloving or even completely absent. Sometimes this is because we are blinded by our attachments; we are so preoccupied—our attention is so kidnapped by our compulsions—that we tune out the background of God's love. I am convinced that our brain cells do, in fact, *habituate* to the constant reality of God's love. We may want to notice divine love, but we ignore it like we ignore our own breathing, in favor of the things that have captured us.[6]

Many other reasons exist for our lack of appreciation of God's constant love. Sometimes the activity of grace so transcends our understanding that it becomes essentially invisible to us. We cannot notice God's loving presence because it is too numinous, too elusively mystical to be perceived. There are also occasions when we cannot appreciate grace because we really do not want to. If God has not lived up to our expectations of how a true lover should act, for example, we may stifle our awareness because of anger or because we want to protect ourselves from being hurt again. And sometimes, as I have indicated, God actively hides grace from us. But of all the possible explanations for our lack of awareness of grace, there is *no* possibility of God being indifferent, or falling in love with someone else instead of us, or pouting because of some insult, or being otherwise elsewhere attached.

The immanent God in us becomes wounded with us, suffers, struggles, hopes, and creates with us, shares every drop of our anger and sadness and joy. The reality of God is so intimate as to be experientially inseparable from our own hearts. But that very same God is at once transcendent, the creating, sustaining, and redeeming Power over and above all things. We should not be dismayed that God's being surpasses understanding, for it is precisely through this mystery that God incarnate can both lovingly share our condition and powerfully deliver us from it. It is through this mystery that grace remains absolute, permanent, and victorious.

Undergirding God's mysterious love for us as individuals is the even more wondrous way grace comes to us in community. I spoke with some facility about how our brain cells form societies and systems, how we ourselves are parts of larger systems, and how our actions reverberate throughout the world. But my language and thought become numb as I look at grace in the systems of humanity. I turn to the cosmic language of John's prologue with which I opened this chapter, to the image of light, to the life that was the light of humanity, a light no darkness can overcome, a living glory endlessly overflowing with love and grace.

"*We* saw its glory," says this ancient hymn. Not "I," but "we." It is a song of community. The soul and God are in love like planet and sun, but the family of humanity is perfused by an intergalactic radiance of grace, a power so immense and dynamic, a Word spoken and so cosmically expanded that time and form, space and substance become simultaneously meaningless and filled with burning glory. At intersections of paths through space that only God can chart, we are drawn together in systems of shared histories, we form covenants, and we become traditions, churches, communities of faith. Here our energies coalesce, and grace pours through the spaciousness of our communal solitude, through our intimacy and interdependence, and, with exponential brilliance, through the sacramental gatherings of true community.

Countless attempts have been made to express the wonder of this mystery. One, by the eighteenth-century evangelist John Newton, speaks simply of the protection and guidance of grace for individuals and of the glory of grace in community. It was to become the most famous folk hymn of modern times, "Amazing Grace":

'Tis grace that brought me safe thus far, and grace will lead me home. When we've been there ten thousand years, bright shining as the sun, We've no less days to sing God's praise, than when we first begun.

Living into Grace

My attempts to express some qualities of grace here have been entirely made of images, and quite wordy ones at that. Poets and artists do better than I at finding representations for grace, but even with the best of all our attempts, grace remains amazing. No words, parables, metaphors, or artistic creations can do justice to its glory. Grace is only truly appreciated and expressed in the actual, immediate experience of real life situations. Finally, it can only be "lived into."

Living into the mystery of grace requires encountering grace as a real gift. Grace is not earned. It is not accomplished or achieved. It is not extracted through manipulation or seduction. It is just given. Nothing in our conditioning prepares us for this radical reality. Some would say that early childhood experience with our parents is important in determining how we come to accept grace in later life. If we had loving, trustworthy parents rather than rejecting or unreliable ones, we would grow up more willing to accept God's grace as a gift. I do not think this is so. We *all* have trouble accepting the radical giftedness of God's grace, no matter what our childhood experience. God's grace is simply not part of our conditioning. Nor can we make it so, though we are sure to try. All our attempts to control the flow of grace will be frustrated because, like God, grace will not become an object for attachment.

Because grace is a pure gift, the most meaningful of our encounters with it will probably come at unintended times, when we are caught off-guard, when our manipulative systems are at rest or otherwise occupied. But still we can pray for grace, actively seek it, and try to relax our hands to receive it.

Prayer for a true gift is a very simple thing—just expressing our desire with no making of deals, no marketing, no manipulation. As the giver of grace, God deserves a straightforward request. As children of God, we have the right to make that request. We can also search for grace, in both obvious and hidden places. The obvious places, which we might avoid or embrace depending on our religious conditioning, include the sacraments, Scripture, and community of our faith, as well as personal prayer and meditation. The hidden places include times of turmoil and failure, encounters with people we dislike, daily drudgery, boredom, and, of course, our addictions. And as we pray and search, we can try to relax our hands to receive grace as a gift. In the middle of beautiful times or ugly ones, peaceful situations or strife, we might just pause, take a breath, and relax. In this little pause, we can look around for God's love, or we can at least remember it.

But living into grace does not depend upon simple receptivity alone. It also requires an active attempt to live life in accord with the facts of grace, even when we do not sense them directly. The facts of grace are simple: grace always exists, it is always available, it is always good, and it is always victorious. For me, living into grace means trying to act on the basis of these facts. I do not do well at it.

My life has given me plenty of real evidence for the facts of grace, and they are certainly verified in my prayer. But whenever I try to live in accord with them it seems I am taking a risk. The risk, of course, is to my addictions; if I try to live in accord with grace, then I will be relinquishing the gods I have made of my attachments. Grace threatens all my normalities. In defense, I am likely to try to distort what I know about the facts of grace or forget them entirely. Thus I must make conscious efforts of will; I must struggle with myself if I am going to act in accord with those facts. Living into grace requires taking risks of faith.

Risks of Faith

Several times now I have said that our real hope lies in that no matter how oppressed we may be, we always retain some spark of capacity to choose. We can use the ember of freedom to choose: to risk ourselves in the goodness of God or to continue to strive for our own autonomy or to give in to the powers that oppress us. I am convinced that nothing whatsoever determines the choices we make at this primal level. Here, finally, the choices are totally up to us; we really are free.

Ironically, freedom becomes most pure when our addictions have so confused and defeated us that we sense no choice left at all. Here, where we feel absolutely powerless, we have the most real power. Nothing is left in us to force us to choose one way or another. Our choice, then, is a true act of faith. We may put our faith in ourselves or in our attachments or in God. It is that simple.

At this level, faith has surprisingly little to do with what we believe in terms of dogma, doctrine, conditioning, or training. Beliefs have prepared a foundation for the choices we make, but at this abject level we are as free from our prior conditioning as we are from our immediate attachments. In such moments, faith is determined by nothing, forced by nothing, and conditioned by nothing. Faith choices are enacted through the cellular activity of our brains, but they are *not predetermined* by that activity. There is no evidence that they are predestined in any way by other cellular patterns.[7]

Here our freedom is always pure, and in this purity faith is always an act of will. But God is not absent; God's grace is more radiant than ever at such times. Its preservation of our freedom becomes most clear when all our other props are taken away. We can even say some inspiration of grace enables us to choose rightly in such situations, for we can pray, like the father of the epileptic boy prayed to Jesus: "I have faith, help my lack of faith." But we must understand that our enabling is pure invitation and empowerment. Grace empowers us to choose rightly in what seem to be the most choiceless of situations, but it does not, and will not, determine that choice.[8]

For this reason, the purest acts of faith always feel like risks. Instead of leading to absolute quietude and serenity, true spiritual growth is characterized by increasingly deep risk taking. Growth in faith means willingness to trust God more and more, not only in those areas of our lives where we are most successful, but also, and most significantly, at those levels where we are most vulnerable, wounded, and weak. It is where our personal power seems most defeated that we are given the most profound opportunities to act in true faith. The purest faith is enacted when all we can choose is to relax our hands or clench them, to turn wordlessly toward or away from God. This tiny option, the faith Jesus measured as the size of a mustard seed, is where grace and the human spirit embrace in absolute perfection and explode in world-changing power.

Trust

I said that our prior conditioning lays a foundation for faith choices but does not determine them. Our foundation contains many elements: education, belief systems, basic attitudes toward life, and so forth. Its strongest element is trust. Trust and faith have a special relationship; trust supports faith, and faith builds trust.

If I climb out on a strange limb, I choose to risk that the limb will be strong enough to hold me. This is an act of faith. If I have been out on that limb before, and it has held me, I will have some trust in it. I will still need to make the choice of faith that the limb has not weakened since the last time, but I face less of a risk because of my preexisting trust. In the language we have been using, trust is conditioned by prior experience. Faith looks to trust and often chooses to rely on it, but it is always taking a risk. Trust is conditioned. Faith is unconditioned.

We may have been taught that grace is present, available, and victorious, and we can try to believe it is true, but it is only through risking it in actual life situations that we give substance to our belief. As we risk believing, and survive, we learn that what we risked was true. Then, when the next opportunity for risking comes along, we will find ourselves a little less fearful. In this way, faith becomes trust.

In many ways, building trust through repeated risks of faith is no different from many other processes of learning. We repeat a behavior, find it good and trustworthy, and the cells of our brains become more accepting of it. Then, as our trust grows, it becomes easier to take the next risk of faith. We learn from experience that God is good because we have risked that God is good. We learn that our most basic desires are trustworthy because we have risked that they were. But because real risking in faith can occur only in those areas of life where we feel most impoverished and vulnerable, it never becomes something we are really comfortable with. For each layer of trust that builds up, another, more challenging risk is offered. True faith choices therefore always feel like risks; they just go on, involving deeper and deeper levels of our being. Each choice remains difficult; what really becomes conditioned in this process is simply our willingness and readiness to *take* the risks of faith. They never stop feeling like risks.

Faith and Addiction

The measure of faith, then, is the degree to which one is really willing to risk the truth of grace. Our past experiences can give us courage to trust in God. Trust can be comforting and consoling in all of life. But faith never rests for long in comfort and consolation. As we grow in trust, we find ourselves challenged to risk more and more of who we are to God's love. For each flower of faith that grows into the fruit of trust, another bud of faith appears, opening into yet another challenge. For this reason, authentic faith can never become an attachment.

We can form images of faith, just as we make images of God or of grace, that will allow us to escape the feeling of risk. Faith images can and do become objects of attachment. When we substitute images of faith for the real thing, as we all often do, we engage in superstition. I want to believe that if I do a certain thing, God will respond in a certain way. So I choose to believe it, and I choose to act on it. But if things do not work out the way I expect, I deny or rationalize the results so that I can continue to cling to my belief. When we become addicted to such comfortable, self-serving images of faith, we are likely to defend and promote them with a desperate aggressiveness. We are threatened by people who believe differently, and we are compelled to convert them, or to isolate ourselves from them, or, as a last resort, to silence them. From one perspective, this is what happened to the man Jesus. He threatened powerful people's addictions to frozen images of faith. They tried to ignore him, but his power had captured too many people's attention. They sought to convert him, but instead he made them painfully aware of their own hypocrisy. In the end they tried to silence him, and that was when God spoke with the loudest voice of all. Similar things happen, I think, whenever images of faith that are objects of attachment come up against true faith.

It is through faith, then, that we can most directly influence the flow of our encounters with grace. Faith is the human component of that mysterious interweaving of divine grace and human intention that can vanquish the power of attachment. Because of their intimate interweaving, we can say that faith is empowered by grace and built on trust, yet simultaneously faith is the most truly independent and unconditioned action available to human free will. The precious intimacy of human will and divine grace simply cannot be appreciated if one approaches it with an either/or mind. True faith choices, those that reflect the purest human freedom, are made in the heart; they are unique products of both what is most human about us and what is most divine about God.

Our language, built as it is on hard subject/object and either/or distinctions, can never do justice to this reality. Yet we all have some experience of it. It is what accounts for the very best decisions we have made in life, the choices that we simply know are right and yet that somehow cannot be logically justified. Sometimes we call such choices "intuitive" because they often seem to be given to our consciousness from a level deep within us that is not purely rational. But the word *intuitive* is also misleading because in popular usage it simply means a hunch, an impulse that comes from somewhere other than our logical mind. In this sense, we are exposed to a wide variety of intuitions coming from many sources within ourselves, the majority of which are far removed from the spiritual truth of our heart. Thus one can never justify choices on the basis that they come from intuition. It may be that what comes from the spiritual heart does seem intuitive, but all that seems intuitive does not necessarily come from the heart.[9]

In truth, authentic faith choices can never be justified on any basis. We may try to articulate and examine them, and it is wise to test them against the rational and the known, but we cannot justify them. We can never adequately explain why we make such choices. This is another reason they feel so risky. We are completely responsible for them, as for all the choices we make, but true faith choices can never be rationalized; nothing can stand as their excuse. A good example can be found in the accounts of Jesus being challenged by religious authorities. He had said who he was, and he had proclaimed his teachings unequivocally. But when the chief priests and elders asked him by what authority he acted, he responded only by asking them the same kind of question. "If you answer this question, I will tell you my authority for acting like this. John's baptism, what was its origin, heavenly or human?" He had put them in the same bind in which they had tried to trap him, and they could not respond. When phrased in either/or terms, such questions are always unanswerable.[10]

Similarly, we cannot pin down where true faith comes from. We can truthfully say it comes from God, for God empowers our faith. But we can just as truthfully say it comes from ourselves, for it represents absolute human freedom. Or we can say, as I have tried to do, that it comes from a mysterious coinherence of grace and will. This may be closer to the truth, but it is just as far away from any possibility of justification.

We all experience heart level choices from time to time. It is in the realm of our most severe addictions, however, that we experience them most clearly and profoundly. We have all had the experience of struggling to break a habit, failing repeatedly, and then at some point meeting with success. What was this success, and how did it happen? We can say it was willpower, but what suddenly empowered our will? We can say it was finding the right strategy, but what enabled that discovery? Did we do it on our own, or did grace break through and deliver us, or was it some mysterious cooperation of will and grace that we could never have engineered?

I cannot further describe how these grace-full choices happen. I can only say that while God is intimately with us in them through our own hearts and those of people around us, we are also very much on our own. Our usual props and handholds are absent, and we are, therefore, very vulnerable. In this vulnerability we are also more dependent upon and open to grace than at any other time.

Desert and Garden

In Scripture, nothing portrays our vulnerability to grace more profoundly than the imagery of the desert and the garden. Here, as I have said, Eden represents the garden that is both our birthplace and our destiny, our home and our promised land. Humanity's struggle with addiction is a journey through the wilderness of idolatry where temptations, trials, and deprivations abound, but where God's grace is always available to guide, protect, empower, and transform us.

The most powerful scriptural metaphor for our journey is the desert sojourn of the Hebrews. God led the people of Israel out of slavery toward the promised land, but their journey took them through great deprivations. In the desert they expressed all the characteristics of addiction and of the addicted personality to a degree that was as agonizing for God and as frustrating for Moses as it was for themselves. They experienced the stress and fear of withdrawal symptoms, longing for the old days of slavery. They hoarded more of their manna than they needed, and it rotted. They deceived themselves with idolatry and excuses. They made resolutions to obey God's commandments, only to apostasize when left to themselves. Their attention was so kidnapped that they became lost in idol worship while surrounded by enemies. They acted in self-centered, narcissistic, manipulative ways, with self-images so eroded that at times they wished they had died in slavery. Yet through it all, God guided the people of Israel, protected them, suffered over them, commanded them, and raged at them, continually inviting and empowering them to choose to trust and to love.[11]

The desert is where battle with attachment takes place. The saga of the desert tells of a journey out of slavery, through the desert, toward the garden that is home. But it is much more than a journey; it is the discovery of the depths of weakness, the power of grace, and the price of both. Moreover, what takes place in the desert is not simply difficult travel and adventurous learning; it is repentance and conversion, the transformation of mixed motivations into purified desire, the greening of desert into garden through the living water of grace. There is no geographic journey here; it all takes place within our hearts. And what happens is not only purgation and purification, but also a loving courtship, a homemaking between the human soul and its Creator.

Out of Slavery

Just as no one escapes addiction, no one can completely avoid encounters with the desert. We may choose these encounters willingly, as when we struggle with a particularly distressing addiction. Perhaps we are trying to quit smoking or drinking because that habit is damaging our health or relationships. Maybe we wish to stop biting our nails because it embarrasses us. Or we may try to diet to lose weight or try to conquer a fear of flying because it is hampering our livelihood. These are expedient, utilitarian motivations, aimed toward a more healthy and efficient life.

Or we may freely choose to enter a desert as part of an intentional spiritual journey. In this case we enter in response to an invitation; we have been called to struggle against all our idolatries, and we have said yes to the call. We have claimed our spiritual longing, and our hope is to be freed from having to cling to anything as a substitute for God. Although we may focus temporarily on particular attachments through fasting, charitable giving, or other ascetic practices, our endeavors are not merely ends in themselves. They are also ways of seeking to deepen our responsiveness to God and God's will.

At other times, however, we find ourselves forced into a desert against our will. Alcohol, narcotic, and other drug addictions can bring people to the desert by eroding their lives until it seems the only alternative to the desert is death. Major addictions of life-style, mood, and relationship can do the same thing. But the plain circumstances of life will also force us into deserts. We will enter a desert of grief when someone or something to which we have become attached is taken away from us. It may be a desert of fear, when a powerful addiction is threatened. Or it may be a desert of pain and humiliation, when in one way or another our attempts to play god have met with defeat.

Thus the deserts of our lives may be large or small, chosen or forced, brief or prolonged. Yet all of them have similar terrain; they all will involve struggle with addiction, and they all will have spiritual significance. Each will be an opportunity for freedom from slavery; each has the potential for becoming a garden. As we have seen, any sincere battle with a particular addiction is likely to bring us to some kind of spiritual confrontation, and any sincere spiritual journey is certain to involve very practical struggles with addictions. Thus no matter how we enter our deserts, we will find ourselves on common ground.

Through the Desert

Any struggle with addiction is a desert because it involves deprivation. If our motivations are primarily utilitarian, this deprivation may consist only of the denial of one specific object of attachment: trying to do without so much food, trying to give up tobacco, and so on. With major addictions or more conscious spiritual motivations, the desert can grow to encompass all of life: every habit may be exposed to the searing, purifying sun; every false prop is vulnerable to relinquishment; and one can be left truly dependent upon the grace of God for sustenance.

Most of our deserts lie somewhere between these extremes, and most of the time we do little more than dance around their edges. All the same, deserts enrich our lives immeasurably. Each desert holds seeds of repentance, possibilities of recognizing how mixed our motives really are. And, with the rain of grace, each desert holds the possibility of our reclaiming our true heart's desire. Even if we only touch their edges, our deserts teach us about the limits of our personal power and point us toward that constant center of ourselves where our dignity is found in our dependence upon God.

Toward Home

Let us never forget that deserts are gardens of courtship as well as fields of battle. Struggle with attachment can be seen as warfare with an insidious enemy, or it can be seen as a romance in which the soul seeks the beloved one for whom it thirsts. Partly, this is simply a matter of attitude. In another sense, however, the transformation of desert into garden is made possible only by God's grace raining upon the areas of our lives that are truly wastelands. From this standpoint, it is no accident that images of desert and garden should so frequently be counterposed in Scripture: "For God has comforted Zion, and will take pity on all her waste places; Turning her wilderness into an Eden, her desert into the garden of God. Joy and gladness will be found in her, and thanksgiving, and the sounds of singing."[12]

To summarize, the desert is the arena of life where we struggle with addiction, in agonizing warfare or in faith-filled hope, and often in both. It may freely chosen, as part of a willing and intentional process of spiritual homemaking. In this case, the desert might be a real physical wilderness that one chooses to enter, as did the desert fathers and mothers of the first centuries of Christianity. Or this chosen desert may exist entirely within one's soul, as it has for countless spiritual pilgrims in their individual and corporate ascetic practices. Or one may be led into a desert that is not of one's own choosing, as in the exile of Israel or the countless deprivations of addiction that are thrust upon us in the course of normal life.

External or interior, chosen or not, the desert is characterized by a soul suffering from withdrawal symptoms, a mind and body deprived of false securities and therefore left to explore the mystical terrain of personal willpower and divine grace. At its mildest, the desert is a laboratory where one learns something about addiction and grace. In more fullness, it is a testing ground where faith and love are tried by fire. And with grace, the desert can become a furnace of real repentance and purification where pride, complacency, and even some of the power of attachment itself can be burned away, and where the rain of God's love can bring conversion: life to the seeds of freedom.[13]

The battle of the desert is waged, the courtship engaged, for no less a prize than where our true treasure will be stored up, and therefore where our hearts will be. The people of Israel were led through their geographic desert three thousand years ago, and, as a people, they have been through countless deserts since then. Moses, their long-suffering leader, went into the wilderness alone many times. So did Elijah and other great Hebrew prophets. So did the great saints of Hinduism, and Gautama the Buddha, and John the Baptist, and the Christian desert mothers and fathers, and Muhammed, and so have countless pilgrims of all religions through the centuries. For modern pilgrims, the geographic desert often takes the form of temporary silent solitude at a simple yet comfortable retreat center or hermitage. For all, however, the desert of the heart remains unchanged. It is not comfortable.

The Desert Experience of Jesus

The New Testament accounts of Jesus' forty days of temptation in the wilderness are an intentional parallel to the Hebrews' forty years of exodus. Jesus is led into the desert by the Holy Spirit. There, while hungry and vulnerable, he is tempted by Satan. He responds to Satan's temptations out of his own freedom and faith, and he is protected by angels. Satan is then defeated, temporarily, and Jesus comes forth for his ministry.[14]

The three temptations Satan offers Jesus consist of the precise themes I have presented as consequences of attachment. First, Satan suggests that Jesus satisfy his hunger by turning stones into bread. This invitation is remarkably similar to the one the serpent gave to Eve: to play god by using autonomous personal power, and to seek satisfaction through something other than God. Failing at this, Satan next tempts Jesus to manipulate God's power for the sake of his own self-indulgence, by jumping off the temple parapet. Here the invitation is to test rather than trust God, to use God superstitiously, as a puppet. Failing once more, Satan proposes the last temptation: he offers Jesus the entire world if he will make Satan his god. This is, of course, the ultimate invitation to idolatry.

Throughout these temptations, Satan was hoping Jesus would fall prey to attachment: attachment to meeting his own needs, attachment to his own power, or attachment to the material riches of the world. Like the serpent in Eden, Satan was trying to lure Jesus into the "I can handle it" trap. It was the very real possibility of such attachment that made Satan's invitations absolute threats. Given the power of who Jesus was, perhaps he really *was* able to "handle it." He really could have turned the stones into bread. He really could have proven his identity by jumping from the parapet. And he could indeed have ruled the world had he so chosen. But instead of giving in to the massive power of temptations to attachment, Jesus stood firm in his own freedom and in his faith and in grace.

It is easy to ascribe Jesus' success in the desert to who he was: the chosen one, God incarnate. Seeing him in such magnificence makes it difficult for us to identify with him. But if we think of Jesus as truly human, as a real man who was truly vulnerable to attachment, then the way he responded to Satan's temptations reveals some things that are critically important. In my opinion, Jesus' actions in the wilderness reveal the way through all our deserts, the way home.

First, Jesus stood firm. He met the adversary, faced the temptation, and did not run away or rationalize. He met the challenge as it was. Second, he acted with strength: he claimed and used his free will with dignity. Third, and most important for our culture, *he did not use his freedom willfully.* None of his responses to Satan was his own autonomous creation. Instead, he relied upon the Law: his words to Satan were quotations from Scripture, from the Torah. Herein lies the practical key to the mystery of human and divine will, the essence of dealing with addiction.

Addiction cannot be defeated by the human will acting on its own, nor by the human will opting out and turning everything over to divine will. Instead, *the power of grace flows most fully when human will chooses to act in harmony with divine will.* In practical terms, this means staying in a situation, being willing to confront it as it is, remaining responsible for the choices one makes in response to it, but at the same time turning to God's grace, protection, and guidance as the ground for one's choices and behavior. It is the difference between *testing* God by avoiding one's own responsibilities and *trusting* God as one acts responsibly. Responsible human freedom thus becomes authentic spiritual surrender, and authentic spiritual surrender is nothing other than responsible human freedom. Here, in the condition of humble dignity, the power of addiction can be overcome.

7. EMPOWERMENT: Grace and Will in Overcoming Addiction

> They were more astonished than ever, saying to one another, "In that case, who can be saved?" Jesus gazed at them and said, "By human resources it is impossible, but not for God, because for God everything is possible."
>
> THE GOSPEL ACCORDING TO MARK

For the power of addiction to be overcome, human will must act in concert with divine will. The human spirit must flow with the Holy Spirit. Personal power must be aligned with the power of grace. How does this happen? It is surely impossible by autonomous willpower alone; the addicted systems of the brain are too numerous and overwhelming. It is also impossible if there is only an intellectual attempt to align the will with grace. Grace is simultaneously too close and too transcendent for comprehension by the intellect. The alignment of our will with God's must happen at a heart level, through authentic choices of faith that are empowered by God.

We cannot make this empowerment happen. But, as I have said, we can pray for it, seek it actively, open our hands for it, and try our best to live it. We can confront our addictions as honestly as possible; we can claim responsibility for the choices we make, and we can turn to God. It is the best way we can reach out for God with humble dignity, the most effective means by which we can nourish our receptivity and responsiveness to grace.

Insofar as we can turn to God, it is grace that enables us to do so. Grace enables dignity within us by empowering our efforts to be honest and responsible. Grace enables humility within us by empowering our realization that our efforts are

insufficient by themselves. Grace enables receptivity and responsiveness within us by empowering our growing trust and
our willingness to take the risks of faith. All this grace comes
from God—God in immanence moving gently in us, and God
in transcendence reaching out to us in radiant love.

Asceticism

In spiritual traditions, human attempts to receive and respond to grace are called *asceticism*. The word comes from the
Greek *askēo*, "to exercise"; it refers to all the authentic intentions
and efforts we make toward fulfilling our deepest desire for
God. Asceticism is our willingness to enter the deserts of our
lives, to commit ourselves to struggle with attachment, to participate in a courtship with grace. We may choose particular
ascetic practices, or we may simply be willing to be present and
responsible in the deserts we are given. Either way, when rightly practiced, asceticism is the human component of the mysterious incarnate intimacy of human intention and divine grace
which holds the only real hope of victory over attachment.

Like detachment, asceticism is widely misunderstood. It has
often been associated with extremes of self-mortification and
denial of life, excesses that reveal a kind of attachment to nonattachment. It is not surprising that such excesses have received
the most publicity over the ages. But by its very nature, authentic asceticism is usually quite ordinary, not very exciting at all.
Jesus' example and the examples of many desert fathers and
mothers provide a vision of what asceticism can be at its best.
It affirms authentic life in grace, nourishes joy and freedom in
the spaciousness of God's love, and enhances authentic passion
to the very limits of our capacity to bear it.[1]

There was in Jesus a wonderful playfulness and encouragement to enjoy God's creation. He ate, drank, and joined cele-
brations; he wept, raged, and joked. He had favorite particular
friends and appreciated the attention and love they gave him.
He saw no reason for his people to fast as long as he was with

them. He complained that neither his own way of life nor the more austere asceticism of John the Baptist could satisfy people's expectations. "For John came, neither eating nor drinking, and they say, 'He is possessed.' Now I come, eating and drinking, and they say, 'Look, a glutton and a drunkard.'"[2]

But Jesus had his asceticism. He had his chosen deserts of solitude and prayer and of tolerating the confusions and misunderstandings of his disciples. And he had the deserts he was led to: the wilderness, Gethsemane, the cross. He was willing to enter them all and to be himself in them, honestly, responsibly, and in faith.

By words and example, Jesus taught the path of authentic asceticism. He explained why people engage in ascetic excesses. Such excesses can happen because of attachment to the letter rather than the meaning of the law, as in Jesus' hilarious description of religious leaders diligently straining gnats out of their cups only to wind up swallowing camels. Ascetic excesses can also happen because of attachment to pride, a desire to show off one's holiness. Jesus told his disciples to give alms in secret and to pray in private. Excesses can also come from thinking that the real enemy is not attachment but the objects to which one becomes attached. "It is not what goes into a person's mouth that defiles," he said, "but what comes out."[3]

Most importantly, Jesus taught that no asceticism, however well it might be practiced, can be the source of liberation. Asceticism does require real dedication of human will, repentance from idolatry, and willingness to relinquish all for God, but the practices only prepare the ground of the heart. Salvation comes by grace, and through faith. True liberation comes not just from a purified heart, but when that heart says yes to God's "Follow me."

Resistance

Now, once again, it is time for confession. I have already admitted I am no victor over my own addictions. Now I must say I am also lousy at asceticism. I have a vision of the ascetic path, and I believe in its truth completely, but I have tremendous difficulty putting it into practice. I do not do well at denying myself the pleasures of my addictions, and it is a major battle for me even to maintain a consistent daily time of prayer. So I feel hypocrisy as I write about asceticism.

In truth, I have never been enamored of asceticism in any form. I much prefer to have my cake and eat it too; I seek God, but I want to do it while I'm indulging in my addictions. Moreover, something in me wants to proclaim that how I am is how I ought to be. Objectively, I cringe when I recall how I have hurt other people by giving in to my addictions, and how those addictions continue to hinder my free availability for others and for God. But subjectively, something in me wants to affirm my broken, imperfect condition.

Similarly, something in me is suspicious of purity and perfection. I have known a few people who thought they were pure and perfect, and I did not like them very much. I also know people who sincerely strive for purity and perfection, and, although I respect them, they scare me. Sometimes I can envision freedom from attachment as a truly liberated and creatively loving state, but at other times it seems more like that old mistaken notion of detachment: austere, deadening, devoid of human caring. In such "freedom," I ask myself, where is the human spirit? Where is the passion? Where is the drive to attain and achieve, to suffer and struggle to create? What happens to the richness that I know as part of this wonderfully imperfect human condition? I could even go so far as to say that freedom from attachment would also mean freedom from needing grace. To put it succinctly, much in me believes we human beings *should* be attached, impure, imperfect.

I have described my feelings as honestly as possible on the chance that you share some of them. In a way this is a trap, for I am certain that these feelings come from a part of me that does not mean well. These feelings arise neither from humility nor common sense, but from the part of me that really is against love, the part that sincerely wants to cling to the slavery of addiction, the part that is terrified by the prospect of being whole, responsible, and free for love.

Let us look more closely at my objections. I say that I want to affirm my brokenness and addiction. To do so would be to honestly choose to remain broken and to want to stay attached. The addicted systems of my brain certainly want to remain that way because that is the normality they are used to. But I have a vision of something better, and when I have my wits about me, I know that only one thing in my brokenness and addiction is good, and that is humility. All the rest keeps me bound and enslaved, and it makes me hurtful to myself and others.

I say that I am suspicious of purity and perfection and afraid of people who strive for them. It is true that I have encountered a few people who have tried to act pure and perfect and who, of course, weren't. But to base fundamental attitudes on such encounters would be ridiculous. And of course I am afraid of true purity and perfection, for along with offering hope for freedom and love they also promise that my willful autonomy will be stripped away. We are all afraid of authentic purity; this is why we put truly holy people on pedestals, to keep them beyond our reach, beyond any possibility that we might be called to be like them. It is also why we isolate such people in society and why we sometimes kill them.

I say that detachment sometimes sounds like an empty, uncreative, and deadening state. If I seek evidence for this, however, I find that nothing could be further from the truth. I can look at the life of Jesus or at the lives of the most truly free people I know, or I can simply reflect upon the tastes of real spiritual freedom I have experienced in my own life. Always the evidence is the same: true freedom from attachment is characterized by great unbounded love, endless creative energy, and deep pervasive joy. Nor need I worry about freedom from addiction taking suffering or caring out of life, for compassion takes the place of attachment. Where there was the agony of clinging to and grasping one's own attachments, freedom brings a feeling of unity with the pain of the world. I think we have all had tastes of this. It is a clean, bright pain. In a way it is more deep and sharp than any addiction agony, because it is so real. But there is no despair in it. It is filled with hope.[4]

Finally, I say that freedom from attachment would mean freedom from needing grace, that it would take away my precious dependency upon God. Is love meant to end when courtship becomes marriage? Of course not. We need God's grace to help us through the deserts of addiction, but that is only one small aspect of grace. Homecoming is only the beginning of homemaking. Grace exists for the fullness of love and for the creative splendor that such fullness brings. There are gardens to create, to dance in. There is pure love to be enjoyed as an end in itself. There are Edens, where people and God simply please one another. And there are the deserts of others, where we can be a part of God's rain. Finally, there are always other deserts in ourselves. I am certain that no one, no matter how holy, is ever completely freed from attachment in this life. The pilgrimages of addiction and grace, the joys and pains of homecoming and homemaking are processes that go on and on. Longing and grace grow into love; love invites communion; communion grows into union; union brings forth creation; creation enables love; love becomes grace and longing.[5]

No, my resistances to freedom are groundless. Their only basis is in the very attachments they are trying to preserve. In the last analysis, they are only mind tricks. In fact, they are old, familiar, and not even very inventive mind tricks. To affirm brokenness and attachment is to deny that a problem exists. To try to have my cake and also eat it is a delaying tactic. To disparage freedom is an attempt to avoid the inevitable withdrawal symptoms that signal freedom's dawning. To say I need to be attached in order to be creative is to rationalize my addiction. To claim that freedom would remove my need for grace is so absurd as to border on the psychotic. Taken all together, these feelings are saying, "I can handle it." When it boils down to this, I must in all conscience give myself the challenge that naturally follows: "If you really do think you can handle it, then go ahead and try." Most of us, most of the time, accept this challenge without even thinking about it. We begin our struggles with addiction by trying to handle them ourselves.

Reformation of Addictive Behavior

In writing the above account of my rationalizations and resistances, I did some difficult self-reflection. Most of the time, we do not do this; we simply struggle with our addictions. I also looked at addiction from a spiritual point of view, with an eye to its heart-level significance. Most of us do not do this either, at least in the beginning. At the outset, most of us tackle an addiction simply because it is giving us trouble, and our only conscious desire is to be rid of it. We want to change a specific addictive behavior, and that alone is challenge enough.

If my primary desire, as best I know it, is simply to change a troublesome addictive behavior, I will hardly be interested in giving my life to God in order to do so. Why should I embark on a spiritual journey that threatens the foundations of all my normalities when the only thing I want is to quit smoking or to stop harassing my spouse or to lose a few pounds? To bring complicated spiritual matters into my struggle can distract me from my primary resolve. I might even use spiritual considerations to avoid quitting the behavior. Such a tactic is certainly possible. I have said before that the only way to break an addiction's power is to stop engaging in the behavior. Anything more complicated is likely to turn into a mind trick.

Every sincere battle with addiction begins with an attempt to change addictive behavior. Literally, we try to *reform our behavior*, substituting constructive actions for destructive ones. In the process, we will have opportunities to notice the spiritual significance of our struggles; we will be invited toward something deeper. If we say yes to that invitation, it means we are willing, at least to some extent, for God to *transform our desire*. But we are not obliged to say yes. Any struggle to reform addictive behavior will surely lead us into a desert, but we are never required to participate in turning that desert into a spiritual garden. It is entirely possible to traverse the outskirts of that desert and emerge with some degree of control over our addictive behavior. I myself stopped smoking this way several times. Most of my friends diet this way, and I know many who have changed phobias, habits of depression, sexual preoccupations, and the like.

Reformation of behavior usually involves *substituting* one addiction for another, adapting to a new, possibly less destructive normality. Sometimes substitution is intentional, sometimes unconscious. An overeater adapts to jogging and yoga; a smoker adapts to chewing gum or eating; a television addict becomes dependent upon guided meditations; an aggressive person becomes accustomed to ingratiating behavior; an alcoholic becomes addicted to AA. Many substitutions are used intentionally as temporary aids in making the transition from one normality to another. They are meant to lessen withdrawal symptoms by making the behavioral change as small as possible. If I can gradually shift small segments of my old normality, the addicted systems of my brain will undergo less stress than if I make a sudden radical change. This way of fighting addiction is like weaning; it is an attempt to make the transition to independence as painless as possible. Sometimes it works; often it does not.[6]

In addition to minimizing withdrawal symptoms, the substitution of one normality for another allows us to avoid the open, empty feeling that comes when an addictive behavior is curtailed. Although this emptiness is really freedom, it is so unconditioned that it feels strange, sometimes even horrible. If we were willing for a deeper transformation of desire, we would have to try to make friends with the spaciousness; we would need to appreciate it as openness to God.

Because openness to God is threatening, and because our desire is more to overcome an addiction than to claim our deeper desire for God, we fill the space with something else. In so doing, we assent to continued slavery under a new master who, we hope, will be kinder. Two risks accompany our choice. First, if the new normality is indeed kinder, it will almost surely seem insufficient. Something in us will continue to remember the old addiction and the greater satisfaction it gave. I was able to quit smoking for two years by means of reformation, but during that entire time nothing quite took the place of cigarettes; I always wanted one. Eventually I caved in and began to smoke again.

Second, there is no guarantee that our new master will be kinder than the old. It might turn out to be worse. Some alcoholics have encountered serious trouble by substituting tranquilizers and sedatives for alcohol. One friend of mine had a heart attack in an overzealous attempt to substitute exercise for food. Another person became psychotic after trying to substitute extreme spiritual practices for her habitual avoidance of problems. Still another, trying to control his anger, substituted a calmness that was achieved by massive repression. His anger broke forth in episodes of physical violence. Eventually he became alcoholic.

Examples like this make it clear that we should be very careful in choosing substitute addictions. Sadly, however, most of these substitutions are made without any reflection whatsoever. The person's only concern is to stop the original addictive behavior; selection of substitutions is left to chance. Chance, in this case, is the haphazard adjustments of deprived cell systems. They will find a new normality, but who is to say whether this normality will be better? Even with careful, conscious reflection, the choice of substitute addictions is not easy. No matter how carefully we make the transition from one normality to another, we will experience withdrawal symptoms and mind tricks. Our private judgment in such things is always impaired. For this reason, if for no other, we should not try to change a major addiction by ourselves. Even if we do not admit needing the empowerment of grace, we should at least admit needing the gracious counsel of other people.

Under the best of circumstances, with good judgment, real dedication, constructive counsel from others, and with grace acknowledged or hidden, substitution of addictions can "work." The old behavior can be reformed, and the new normality can be a better one. The underlying processes of attachment remain, requiring continued vigilance, but it really can "work." I say "work" because reformation requires effort. But I put the word in quotes because the relationship between effort and success in overcoming addictive behavior is not one of simple cause and effect; the intervening variable is grace.

When reformation "works," it is well worth it. It may even be life saving. But because it applies only to behavior and does not address the underlying processes of attachment, old addictive behavior will tend to resurface at a later date. Even so, we will have had the experience of the struggle, and we will have learned something about ourselves. If our sense of failure does not become a complete mind trick, we may even remember what we have learned. This will stand us in good stead for future struggles; it will allow us to step further into the next desert. We will be that much closer to making friends with spaciousness, to recognizing God's inevitable homeward call, the invitation to the transformation of our desire.

Consecration and the Transformation of Desire

Every struggle with addiction, no matter how small, and no matter what our spiritual interest may be, will include at least brief encounters with spaciousness. Through the spaciousness will come some homeward call, some invitation to transformation. If we answer yes, even with the tiniest and most timid voice, our struggle becomes *consecrated*. Consecration means dedication to God. It occurs when we claim our deepest desire for God, beneath, above, and beyond all other things.

Everything we do involves some kind of dedication. When we simply try to reform a troublesome addiction, our struggle is dedicated to minimizing the pain that addiction causes us and others. But in consecration we dedicate our struggle to something more; consecration is our assent to God's transforming grace, our commitment homeward.

In the beginning, we will not understand the full meaning of consecration. Perhaps, in this life, we never will. Nor will we comprehend the ups and downs, the joys and agonies of the journey that must follow. And certainly we will be unable to grasp the overarching cosmic meaning of our small assent, the joy it gives to God, the deepening love it will bring to humanity, the universal covenant it has enriched. We may not have any idea that consecration means encounter with spaciousness, that an unconditioned reality awaits our conditioned mind. But our yes comes from some taste, some bare recollection of all these things. We know it has something to do with home. There is love in it and hope. We feel a small breeze of freedom. And in the tiny space our hearts can say yes.

Through grace, with our assent, our desire begins to be transformed. Energies that once were dedicated simply to relieving ourselves from pain now become dedicated to a larger goodness, more aligned with the true treasure of our hearts. Where we were once interested only in conquering a specific addiction, we are now claiming a deeper longing, and we are concerned with becoming more free from attachments in general, for the sake of love. What had begun as an expedient attempt to reform a behavior has now become a process of transforming a life.[7]

If I let my mind run free with this idea, I find myself asking an absurd question. "If I do say yes to God, if I do consecrate myself, will that help me overcome my addictions?" The question cannot be answered because it contains an impossible contradiction. If I am primarily dedicated to overcoming addiction, I cannot really be consecrated to God. I raise it, however, because it is a very human question. After all, I have said that consecration opens the door to transformation of desire, and transformation does affect our underlying attachments. To make the question seem reasonable, all I have to do is forget that the whole process involves my faithful participation in a mystery that only God can comprehend. We always have to try, it seems, for more mastery than mystery, more manipulation than participation. In me, the question comes from that old "have my cake and eat it" mentality. Here I am wondering if I can get over my addictions by surrendering myself to God. Before, when I was describing my resistances to asceticism, I was wondering if I could surrender myself to God without having to give up my addictions.[8]

In the light of consecration, both of these notions become absurd. Consecration cuts through self-deception; it often reveals more than we wish to know about our motivations. It illuminates the difference between true spiritual searching and expedient, ego-centered enterprises that masquerade in spiritual garb. In modern Western society, many activities are called spiritual because they involve meditation or other ascetic practices taken from spiritual traditions, or because they address psychological and physical issues in particularly profound and integrative ways. But whether they really are spiritual depends upon the dedication of the participant.

Someone may teach me a meditation technique or a method of prayer that will help ease some of the symptoms of my stress addiction. That this technique comes from a spiritual tradition and involves spiritual images does not make it spiritual for me. It becomes truly spiritual only when my effort is consecrated to love and not just dedicated to lowering my blood pressure or the acidity of my stomach. Authentic asceticism is not a collection of practices or insights. It is a condition of the heart. With the willing consecration of the heart, any activity, however mundane, can become ascetic. Without consecration, no activity, however spiritual it may appear, is truly ascetic.

This is not to say, however, that the easing of distress is a bad thing. When I first sensed a difference between true and false asceticism, I made distinctions far too arbitrarily. I was impatient with the confused thinking that calls everything that feels good "spiritual." I grimaced when health professionals asked about using meditation or prayer as "therapeutic adjuncts." I squirmed when a friend said, "I fasted during Lent, and it was a wonderful experience. I lost five pounds." I even found myself rebelling when someone told me how prayer had helped him overcome depression. I wanted to say, "Now, when your depression is gone, where is your prayer?"

But my impatience was caused by my own addiction to precision. Now I'm not quite so attached to making either/or distinctions. Grace, mediated by a fair amount of humiliation, has lightened me up a bit. There is nothing inherently wrong with meditating to lower blood pressure, losing a few pounds during Lent, or using prayer as a technique. In fact, such things can be very right. Grace can call us through all such things, and it is impossible to predict when we will be enabled to say yes. Even if we have never before paused to sense the deeper longing of our hearts, each struggle is an opportunity for growth, a moment where grace can flow. And each real experience of growth brings us closer to seeing who we are, to claiming our desire, to saying yes, to consecration.

In some cases, modern "spiritual" enterprises that pander primarily to ego satisfaction are much more healthy than some old religious ascetic practices that became institutionalized and devoid of any affirmation of goodness. If distortion must occur—and apparently it must—then it is better that the distortions at least encourage life and creation instead of repression and denial.

Deliverance

Grace, thank God, can break through to us regardless of our intent. God graciously awaits our assent and our participation in transformation, but God does not wait to give us good things. No matter what our primary dedication may be at any given time, God's love can burst through upon us, miraculously. In my experience, these special miracles happen with uncommon frequency in the course of addictions. Without any evident reason, the weight of an addiction is lifted. "I was walking to the grocery store one day," said one alcoholic man, "and there, on the sidewalk, I discovered equanimity." He had suffered from alcoholism for many years, and that particular day had seemed no different from any other. Yet in a simple, wondrous moment, his life was transformed. He hasn't had a drink since. He did not describe his experience in religious terms. All he knew was that nothing he had learned, and nothing he had done, had made it happen.

This is the spiritual experience I learned about from recovering addicts, the unique phenomenon that sparked my professional/personal journey into psychology and spirituality. I can only call it deliverance. There is no physical, psychological, or social explanation for such sudden empowerments. People who have experienced them call them miraculous. In many cases these people have struggled with their addictions for years. Then suddenly, with no warning, the power of the addiction is broken. To me, deliverance is like any other miraculous physical, emotional, or social healing. It is an example of "supernatural" or "extraordinary" grace, an obvious intervention by the hand of God in which physical structure and function are changed and growth toward wholeness is enabled. In the case of addiction, healing takes the form of empowerment that enables people to modify addictive behavior.[9]

I am choosing my words carefully here. Deliverance *enables* a person to *make* a change in his or her behavior; in my experience deliverance does not *remove* the addiction and its underlying attachments. Something obviously happens to the systems of the brain when deliverance occurs; either the addicted systems are weakened or the ones seeking freedom are strengthened or both. But there is still a role for continued personal responsibility. Considerable intention and vigilance are still necessary. I have witnessed many healings of substance and nonsubstance addictions and of many other disorders. In none of these miraculous empowerments were people freed from having to remain intentional about avoiding a return to their old addictive behaviors. The real miracle was that avoidance became possible; the person could actually do it. Deliverance does not remove a person's responsibility; it does empower the person to exercise responsibility simply, gently, and effectively.[10]

In a way, this is how grace seems to work with us in all areas of life. The special flowerings of grace that we call deliverance and miracles seem so extraordinary only because of the way we look at them. The natural grace that God continually offers us in the normal circumstances of our lives is really just as miraculous. It stands ready to transform and empower us in the most ordinary situations. Miracles are nothing other than God's ordinary truth seen with surprised eyes.

Our very being in this world, our existence as individuals and communities, is miraculous. It is miraculous that God creates us with bodies and brains that are capable of adapting to virtually any conditions, and that God preserves within us an invincible freedom of choice. It is no more miraculous that God can thaw the most frozen of our adaptations and massively, instantaneously, empower our freedom of choice. A particular eruption of grace strikes into a person's life like a lightning bolt of loving energy; the power of God's goodness shines in victory over a particular human enslavement or misfortune. The enemy is weakened; the person is empowered.

I believe that grace's empowerment is present in all true healings, in deliverances of all kinds, and in any movement toward wholeness and love and freedom, however great or small. It is present in physical and psychological healing, in social and political reconciliation, in cultural and scientific breakthrough, in spiritual deliverance from evil, in religious repentance and conversion, and in the ongoing process of spiritual growth. It is present wherever love really grows. In every such situation, grace enables us to make necessary initial changes and to continue, over time, to nurture those changes in creative, constructive ways.

God does not flash into our lives to work a piece of magic upon us and then disappear. To do so would eradicate human dignity; it would prevent our participation. Instead, God's grace is always present intimately within us, inviting and empowering us toward more full, more free exercise of will and responsibility. The more open and spacious our will and responsibility become, the more God and person commune in creative splendor.

We are never simply visited with a healing or deliverance, which we can then safely forget. Grace is not a pill we are given or a method applied to us so that we can simply go on about our business. Grace always invites us forward. Every liberation requires continued attention, every healing demands continued care, every deliverance demands follow-up and every conversion requires faithful deepening. If we do not respond to these ongoing calls, if we deny our empowerments for continued growth in freedom and responsibility, our healings may well be stillborn. Then, as in Jesus' words about evil spirits returning to a house swept clean, our last condition may turn out to be worse than our first.[11]

Gentle Victories

I have repeatedly emphasized the role of human will in deliverance because it is all too easy to see deliverance as entirely God's business. Similarly, I have emphasized the role of grace in asceticism and reformation because we can be tempted to see them as depending entirely on human effort. I can say with certainty that every authentic movement toward freedom involves both grace and will, but it is impossible to describe just how grace and will interact. If we were to look only at God's transcendence, we could develop an explanation based on God's actions and our responses. Similarly, if we concentrated only on God's immanence, we could develop a psychological explanation based on our journey toward individuation and discovery of the True Self. But God is both immanent and transcendent, so any either/or explanation is bound to be insufficient. We are left with mystery. Here we find another meaning of consecration: the willingness to participate in mystery through faith instead of through comprehension.

Because I cannot explain the coinherence of grace and will, I must turn away from objective discussion and tell some stories instead. I have chosen to relate the experiences of three people who have overcome addiction. These people were not particularly interested in spiritual growth; they simply wanted to be free of their addictions. Their stories reveal the mysterious and gentle ways in which reformation and deliverance interact. All three are success stories because of one fact: the people did not fill up the space left by their addictions. How and why they were empowered to live within this spaciousness remain a mystery.

The man who experienced equanimity on the way to the grocery store was a middle-aged steelworker. He had been struggling with alcoholism for many years. He had reformed his behavior on at least seven occasions and had been dry for as long as eight months at a time. He had been in individual and group psychotherapy and had attended AA. He intellectually understood AA's "surrender to a higher power," but, as he put it, "I never truly knew what it was or how to do it." He had experienced several rock bottoms, but there had been nothing liberating about them. His wife had left him twice because of his drinking, and his grown children seldom visited. He had managed to keep his job, but it was in jeopardy because of his erratic performance. All his attempts to stop drinking had been complicated and turbulent, full of failed resolutions and eroded willpower, replete with self-recriminations and depression. But after that moment on the sidewalk, everything changed. It was not that he decided to quit; it was just that he didn't take the next drink. Discipline was involved and sincere intention, but no resolutions and no willpower. As he described it later, "I didn't fight the desire to drink anymore; I just did not drink."

What had been so complicated now became very simple. Not easy, but simple. And that was it. He continued to go to AA because it helped him stay vigilant. But he did not develop substitute addictions. Where alcohol had been, there was emptiness. He described feeling scared of that emptiness when he would think about it, but he just let it be. Sometimes, when he normally would have been drinking, he just sat and looked at the sky. He did not feel pride about having quit drinking, but he did feel good. His imprisonment was over.

Another middle-aged man, a lawyer, became addicted to a particular sexual relationship. He had long been attracted to a coworker, and, as they worked closely together on an extended project, they fell in love. He kept it all secret from his wife, and he hated the deceit of it, but his lover made him feel "like I was really alive and free for the first time in years." At first it did not seem like an addiction at all, though he could hardly think of anything but her. It was, at first, a real romance. He met his lover once a week; he brought her gifts; she listened to the yearnings of his heart. As time went on, however, he began to feel compelled by the relationship. He craved his weekly fix of self-esteem and sexual release, but he felt depressed after each encounter. There were times when he didn't even want to go but somehow felt he had to. His lover sensed this, and their relationship became turbulent. Countless times they resolved to end the affair, only to wind up back in each other's arms. They sincerely tried to stay apart, but they failed. He prayed for forgiveness and release, but nothing seemed to happen. He became increasingly fearful that his wife would find out or that his lover would become vengeful. He saw a therapist, and he shared his secret with a trusted friend. Neither could help him change his behavior, but they did help him realize that he was more compelled than in love. As time passed, his work suffered. He and his lover talked for hours, trying to find a resolution. Then one day he said to her, "This is the last time I'll be here." "I know," she answered. It was. Afterward, he said, "I just didn't go see her again, that's all. It was hard; I would think of her and wonder about her and remember the times we'd had. But I also knew I was worth more than that, and so was she. I just didn't go back."

An executive became severely addicted to stress. She had always been hard driving and overachieving, but her life had remained in good balance until she was promoted to the head of her office. She leaped into this new position with zeal and accomplished far more than any of her predecessors had. She took her work home with her and often stayed up into the night to finish a project. She worked on holidays and through her vacations. Her husband and children supported this for a while; they had never seen her so full of energy and life. But it went too far. She began to have trouble sleeping at night and found her mind racing at times when she needed to concentrate. She lost her ability to be attentive to her family. When she tried to relax, she became even more jittery. Her friends and family were worried; they told her she had to slow down. She agreed. She joined an aerobics group, but although the exercise made her feel better and helped her sleep, she felt herself becoming more and more fatigued. She took two weeks' vacation but worried constantly about the office. She tried to meditate, but the jangling in her mind nearly drove her crazy. She tried to pick up old hobbies, but they no longer held her interest. She thought she might be headed for a nervous breakdown; there seemed to be nothing she could do. Finally, she began to wonder what it was all for. Nothing seemed worth it. Her success at work was not going to save the world. Her constant activity was hardly making her a better person. Even her struggles to relax were getting her nowhere. Out of this realization, she found herself saying, "I quit." She did not mean she intended to quit striving nor to quit trying to relax nor to quit working nor any other specific thing. "I don't know what I quit," she said, "I just quit." It was completely illogical, and she could not explain it to anyone. Quitting meant not doing anything special, but it also meant doing whatever she needed to do next. It was not a resolution; she just quit. With this decision, she experienced some peace. Her hectic pace continued for a long time, and her mind continued to race. But beneath it, she felt peace. And, over time, as she just did the next thing she needed to do, she slowed down.

Invitation

These three stories portray the mysterious way specific addictions are overcome. Each account includes honest attempts at reformation. Each moves beyond willpower. And each contains at least a degree of deliverance. Somehow, for these three people, it "worked." In each case, the addictive behavior was changed, and there was no substitution. These people are still prone to addiction, as are we all, and they have learned to be especially vigilant where their particular addictions are concerned. But they have indeed been liberated. The steelworker continues to attend AA every month or so; it helps his vigilance. If you ask him, he will say he is a recovering alcoholic, but he doesn't make a big deal of it. He feels the desire for a drink now and then, but, as he says, "I just don't."

The lawyer has found himself attracted to many other women in the years since his affair, but he deals with his attractions quickly and simply. "I start to think about what it would be like with a certain woman, and then I recognize the pattern. I don't fight the fantasy off; I don't try to put it out of my mind. I just don't indulge in it, and it goes away. For a while, I thought I could enjoy the fantasies without acting on them. But it was not sufficient to do that. So I simply notice them and let them pass of their own accord. It's like getting rid of an alley cat. You don't have to kick it; just don't feed it." He says he enjoys the company of women more than ever "now that they are people, not objects."

The executive still has to be careful about overdoing, but she can tell when she starts to rev up. It is a very specific feeling. She describes how it begins: "I notice that I'm getting ahead of the present moment. I am no longer looking at what is; instead,

I'm concentrating on what will be." She identifies this feeling as a danger signal, a sign to take a breath and look around her. Like the other two people, she doesn't try to fight off the rising addictive pattern; she simply doesn't engage in it.

All three people know that they are vulnerable. They could easily fall back into their old addictive behaviors. At times, when they think about it, they feel as if they are walking on a narrow ledge. It would be so easy to fall off. Yet, paradoxically, they rarely find it difficult to remain centered. Somehow they have learned that they can't stay centered by fighting; they stay centered by simply not leaning over the edge.

Even though the three people do not describe their stories in religious terms, the stories reflect a delicate spiritual quality. It has something to do with the simplicity of their intent, the direct vulnerability with which they notice their own minds, and the open present-centeredness they somehow maintain. The qualities come, I am certain, from the fact that these people did not substitute addictions. They encountered spaciousness. And, to a degree, they have made friends with it.[12]

The quality of these stories would have been different if the steelworker had said, "Every time I feel like having a drink I have a cup of coffee instead," and if the lawyer had said, "I just put those sexual thoughts out of my mind," and if the executive had said, "I make sure I meditate twenty minutes every day." Such statements would indicate that the empty spaces had been filled, that the persons were still trying to control their behavior willfully. Instead, the three reflect a transparency, a gentle yet dignified openness to what is real. They are, as I have defined it, contemplative. They have faced life in a truly undefended and open-eyed way.

A contemplative quality can be found in anyone who has encountered emptiness and chosen not to run away. A sense of balance within spaciousness remains within such people, like a window between infinity and the world of everyday experience. They are not only wiser and humbler because of their addictions; they are also more available. Through their spaciousness, they are continually invited homeward. They have, in fact, already begun the homeward journey.

Assent

In a way, such people already have said yes. They may not have thought about it consciously, but something in their hearts was willing to confront the emptiness and to stay with it. Something deep inside them chose not to run away. In each of the three stories, the person chose the way of liberation in a moment of empowerment and continues to choose that way. None of the choices was forced; each person could have returned to the old addictive behavior or substituted another. They still could do this, at any time. That is why they must remain vigilant. But they did choose the way of liberation, and they chose it freely.

To me, it is striking that their choices were so gentle, so plain. With everything I have said about the struggles of the desert, about resistances to asceticism, and about the power of consecration, one would expect such choices to be very dramatic. The yes that the heart speaks to God, we might assume, would be preceded by great intellectual considerations and emotional upheavals and followed by enthusiastic celebration. Yet, in these stories, the yes was so quiet and so simple that it was barely noticed. Could it be that the heart speaks to God sometimes in ways that escape detection by our cellular representations? Is it possible that the heart can begin an act of consecration while the mind is still wondering what it's all about?

By the grace of God, the answer is yes. Of all the spiritual literature I have read, my favorite quotation is a simple one that was written by a very simple person. Brother Lawrence, a seventeenth-century Carmelite friar, worked in the kitchen of his monastery and wrote a few words about practicing the presence of God. Among those words are these: "People would be surprised if they knew what the soul said to God sometimes."[13]

8. HOMECOMING: Discernment and the Consecrated Life

Everyone moved by the Spirit is a child of God. The spirit you received is not the spirit of slaves bringing fear into your lives again; it is the spirit of children, and it makes us cry out, "Abba, Father; Amma, Mother."

PAUL'S LETTER TO THE ROMANS

Consecration is the bridge between reformation and transformation, the integrating choice that assents to God's homeward call. It is impossible to say when consecration actually begins. Those of us who consider ourselves spiritual pilgrims have tried repeatedly to consecrate ourselves on our own terms, and we have failed. But then, often when we have least expected it, we have heard a gentle invitation, and we have claimed a consecration that has already happened in our hearts.

I am sure Brother Lawrence was right; some kind of dialogue with God does go on in our hearts, beyond all our images. I know my own conscious claimings always seem to take place somewhat after the fact. My mind plays catch up with my heart. I may like to think I am autonomously charting my own course, but I keep discovering that my little ship has been answering to deeper, hidden currents all along.

What happens at this deeper level is the most important thing; how we name or understand it is secondary. Because of this, all people, regardless of their intellectual ability, are capable of authentic consecration and transformation. The mentally retarded, schizophrenic, and brain-damaged members of the human family are no less qualified for spiritual growth. In some cases, they are even more blessed. A friend of mine once described a mentally retarded person who came to her for spiritual direction. She said, "There is room in his inn."

Discernment

Those of us with greater intellectual abilities have the capacity for more precise understanding, but our mind tricks are also more inventive, and we more readily fill the holy spaces of our lives with thoughts. There is need for care in how we use our intellects. As we try to claim our consecration, we are faced with serious questions: How do we live out our consecration? How can we participate in harmony with God's transformation of our desire? In the vast arena of our experience, how can we tell the inspirations of love from the temptations of attachment? How can we align our intentions with God's deeper currents? These questions lead us to the territory of spiritual discernment.

Volumes have been written about discernment, and, as a topic for discussion, it can become almost hopelessly complicated. The intellect ties itself in knots trying to comprehend how it can seek the will of God who is wholly other from us and intimately united with us at the same time. Ultimately, however, discernment becomes a way of life, and then it is not so complicated. Discernment means living life prayerfully—bringing oneself to God as honestly and completely as possible, seeking God's guidance as openly as possible, and then, in faith, responding as fully as possible. A life lived this way, trying to bring all one's faculties into harmony with God's transforming grace, is consecration in practice.[1]

I have some things to say about this kind of life, some practical suggestions to make. Once again, however, it is an area I enter with trepidation. There are three reasons for this.

First, in spite of all I have said about the mysterious intimacy of will and grace, I am afraid you will take my suggestions as a "how to" approach. If you are addicted to control as I am, you will want to take specifics and turn them into methods. If you do, the spaciousness will be filled and the mystery will disappear.

Second, in spite of all I have said about God's unconditional love, I am afraid that my comments will engender feelings of success and failure, that they will encourage a preoccupation with "doing it right." Those of us who have substantial religious backgrounds are likely to be addicted to legalism; we look at all spiritual matters through lenses of rightness and wrongness. When this is all we see, grace is eclipsed.

Third, in spite of all the confessions I have made of my own attachments and idolatries, I am concerned that I will sound holier than thou when I make suggestions about living a consecrated life. I do try to live a consecrated life, but as I review the comments I am about to make, I despair of ever living them fully. Let it suffice to say that the suggestions I make are as much for myself as for anyone else.

From all the observations and insights we have covered, I have drawn together five qualities that for me characterize a life lived with consecrated intent. They are characteristics of discernment, things we can do and attitudes we can nurture to help us embrace God's loving activity and join more fully the mystical courtship that is already happening. They are, if you will, guideposts through the desert. They are not the *way* home, but they do point in that direction. These qualities are *honesty, dignity, community, responsibility, and simplicity.*

I will discuss these qualities in the context of addiction because I am convinced that the journey homeward is one of increasing freedom from attachment. What applies to specific addictions applies to life, and vice versa. You will probably find little that is new in these qualities; we have already touched on them in many ways. Members of AA and other "anonymous" groups will find them very consonant with their own twelve steps. Spiritual traditions have been teaching them for millennia, and the behavioral sciences are slowly rediscovering them.

But I hope these qualities will draw the facts and observations we have explored into a more meaningful whole and point toward actions and attitudes that will be helpful. I also hope they will reveal the nature of consecration more clearly. Most of all, I hope they will not interfere with the precious appreciation of that process that is going on right now in your own heart.

Honesty

Honesty means acceptance. We must begin by accepting the fact of our addictedness. To accept this is not to affirm it, but to admit it, to acknowledge that it really exists. In religious language, this kind of acceptance is confession. In the context of a specific addiction, acceptance means acknowledging that a problem exists. In the context of consecration, it means recognizing that our attachments are our idols, that they eclipse God.

Acceptance also implies a certain lack of hysteria. We are bound to feel guilty when we recognize how attached we are. If we do not overcomplicate it, this is a good, solid guilt. It marks the beginning of repentance, the turning back toward our true heart's desire. But to indulge in self-flagellation or endless apologizing is nearly always a ploy. If we keep on fawning about our guilt before our images of God and our own super-egos, we may never get around to stopping the behavior we felt guilty about in the first place. The simple prayer that Jesus taught cuts through all this: "Forgive us our trespasses, as we forgive those who trespass against us. Lead us not into temptation, and deliver us from evil." It is a matter of recognizing where attachment has made us idolatrous and unloving, admitting it, and, with God's help, trying to avoid repeating those behaviors.[2]

With confession and repentance, the battle is waged and mind tricks begin in earnest. Honesty becomes more difficult and, simultaneously, more important. Now honesty involves steadiness. It is a willingness to continue to face the truth of who we are, regardless of how threatening or unpleasant our perceptions may be. It means hanging in there with ourselves and with God, learning our mind tricks by experiencing how they defeat us, recognizing our avoidances, acknowledging our lapses, learning completely that we cannot handle it ourselves. This steady self-confrontation requires strength and courage. We cannot use failure as an excuse to quit trying. We cannot fake surrenders or contrive rock bottoms. All we can do is just stay there, trying to be at least partially as faithful and present to ourselves as God is.

Meditation and quiet, open prayer can help. In one sense, quiet prayer is really nothing other than the practice of faithful attentiveness. I am not speaking here of meditation that involves guided imagery or scriptural reflections, but of a more contemplative practice in which one just sits still and stays awake with God. This kind of meditation is extremely difficult, especially in the midst of battles with addiction, because it gives us nothing special to do, no fancy ways to entertain ourselves or to escape from the simple truth of the moment.[3]

Attentive meditation can be a true ascetic practice. It is like fasting for the mind. One only sits there, inclined toward God, noticing the thoughts and sensations that come and go, adding nothing to them, subtracting nothing from them. The mind is allowed to be what it is, but it is *seen*. When properly practiced and truly graced, this kind of meditation—to the extent that we can bear it—can be very powerful in exposing and vaporizing mind tricks.

Since the sole purpose of mind tricks is to perpetuate attachment, they will always try to compromise our consecration. Ultimately, consecration means death to attachment; it allows no equivocation; it seeks only the fulfillment of the two great commandments. Consecration takes our struggles out of the private, self-centered realm of our own minds and expands them into communal and even cosmic significance. Therefore the addicted systems of our brains will do everything in their power to weaken our sense of consecration. Although they can never completely destroy our basic desire for God, mind tricks can confuse it, distort it, and even make us forget it entirely.

Let me give an example. A few years ago, I became aware of how I habitually use a biting, sarcastic humor to criticize other people. At times I have humiliated people this way. It took me a long time to admit my humor was destructive, but I finally did, and I tried to stop it. But I couldn't stop; I realized it was an addiction. I reflected upon it, journaled about it, and prayed about it. I talked it over with friends. I realized how unloving it was and how selfish, and I saw how it eclipsed my attentiveness to God. I truly felt that God was inviting me to relinquish that behavior, and I truly wanted to relinquish it. To the best of my knowledge, my intent was consecrated.

In trying to stop this behavior, I encountered all the struggles one might expect. I experienced withdrawal symptoms; I felt ill at ease when I didn't do it, and sometimes my anger came out in more direct and harsh ways. I had trouble facing the emptiness left by the removal of this behavior: "If I'm not going to crack a joke at this point, what *am* I going to do?" I decided, almost unconsciously, that when I felt like being sarcastic in a meeting or a conversation, I would pray instead. On the surface, it felt like a nice choice, and it might indeed have been. But my prayer was not a simple, honest turning to God. It did not seek God's help in facing the emptiness left by my addiction. Instead, the prayer itself became a substitute addiction. I could tell when this happened, because the prayer was not sincere; it was not heartfelt; it was routinized and automatic. At the point of prayer, my consecration was distorted. Although I was using a spiritual method, I had made it into my own private technique, a technique that eclipsed both God and others. All I saw was myself against the addiction; grace was no longer in my vision.

Then one day, in a meeting where I had been doing the whole routine, we had a period of silence. As I sat there, truly in prayer for once, I *saw* it. I felt the impulse to say something cynical as it arose. I watched my mind go into its little image of prayer. I felt the constrictedness it brought, the loss of spaciousness. I relaxed, opened, and the "prayer" had vaporized. After that, things were simpler. I'm still addicted to that sarcastic humor. But I caught one mind trick, and I am a little more willing to stay with the spaciousness that is left when I don't engage in the behavior. And my consecration, I think, is a little more clear.

The old desert father Abba Poeman is noted for saying, "Vigilance, self-knowledge, and discernment: these are the true guides of the soul."⁴ Meditation is just one way of facilitating honest self-observation. Daily reflection and journaling are others. Discussion with other people is also critically important. However it comes to us, self-observation is necessary for an honest discernment of our position in relationship to God and attachment.

For example, I do mean it when I pray, "Thy will be done." But at any given time, in relation to a particular attachment, there are limits as to how much of God's will I really want done. Although my cosmic intent is sincerely for God's will, I am not so free when it comes to the small specifics of my life. It is helpful to be as honest as possible, to be able to say, "Thy will be done, but I do want to keep this thing. . . ." There is nothing to be ashamed of in this prayer; it is a matter of bringing ourselves, just as we are, to God, just as God is.

I not only try to pray honestly about my addictions and acknowledge my lack of desire to be free, but I also try to turn to God *while* I am engaging in addictive behaviors. Some of my addictive behaviors are not at all the kind of things one would associate with prayer, so turning to God is difficult. I use this difficulty as a kind of diagnostic aid from time to time: if I find it very hard to bring myself to pray, to honestly turn to God in the midst of a particular activity, it is likely that activity is idolatrous. In most such cases, even if I can turn to God, I cannot honestly pray to be freed from the behavior; I really do not want to give it up. At the very least, however, I can wordlessly turn to God as if to say, "See? This is who I am."

I don't like doing this, and I don't do it very often. I resist this kind of prayer because prayer involves listening, and I might not like what I hear. What if I sense God saying, "It is time, now, for this to go?" The challenge of honesty then becomes, "Are you willing to say no to God? Can you stand up and say, 'I do love you, but I am not ready to let this go'?"

In fact, we have unconsciously been saying no to God in countless areas of our lives all along. Honesty simply asks if we are willing to acknowledge some of this. Can we stop hiding our secret desires and start claiming them openly before God, who, of course, already knows them anyway? Many of the great Old Testament figures had such courage; they argued, refused, and wrestled with God. They stood up for themselves with dignity. It might be called chutzpa, but these people were honest, and God certainly seemed to respect them for it. Jesus stood with dignity also; he was willing for God's will, but he was able to express his own desires.

Honesty before God requires the most fundamental risk of faith we can take: the risk that God is good, that God does love us unconditionally. It is in taking this risk that we rediscover our dignity. To bring the truth of ourselves, just as we are, to God, just as God is, is the most dignified thing we can do in this life.

Dignity

Honesty risks that God is good. Dignity risks that we ourselves are good. Dignity is acting as if we believe the facts of our creation are true: that we are indeed created in God's image, that we are created out of love, that we are good because God created us, and that we have the goodness of God within us. Dignity is risking that, as the popular saying goes, "God don't make junk."

Like honesty, dignity is a choice, a risk of faith. All too often, we think our dignity must depend upon our self-images. Then, when our self-images are lousy, we become depressed. Or

when our self-images are good, we become proud or even grandiose. I have said before that we become addicted to our self-
images, our cellular representations of self. In fact, I think every
self-image represents some degree of addiction. Self-images
have their rightful place in our lives, to be sure. They help us
conceptualize and communicate about ourselves. But nearly always we use those images to fill the spacious mystery of who
we really are. If we do not like one of the images, we will try
to break our addiction to it, but we are very sure to substitute
another. The space left by any relinquished object of attachment
can be threatening, but when it comes to our sense of ourselves, we are terrified. Perhaps in the journey toward freedom,
this is the last addiction to go.

When we are especially attached to a bad self-image and its
associated thoughts and feelings, we call ourselves depressed.
We all know what this kind of depression is like. It is different
from major psychiatric depressions, which stifle life energy. An
addictive depression has an energy all its own; it feeds on itself
and on our attempts to overcome it, just as any addiction does.
And even though it feels awful, we cling to it because it gives
us a solid sense of who we are. We become accustomed to it,
addicted to being depressed. For most of us the attachment is
a transient one that follows certain blows to our egos; we wind
up kicking ourselves out of it before it goes on too long. Others
go into therapy and try to find a somewhat better self-image to
substitute. But some of us make a lifelong habit of it; it's how
we really feel about ourselves, way down deep.

In the larger spiritual journey, significant attachment to any
self-image can be a serious compromise to consecration. Overly
grandiose self-images lead us to feel we have no need for anything beyond our own egos. When this attitude creeps into the
spiritual life, it leads to sorcery and charlatanism. Depressive
self-images say, "You are no good; therefore your consecration
means nothing." It is important to recognize self-commentaries
for the mind tricks that they are. They have nothing to do with
our real dignity, and their only purpose is to keep our attach-

ment to self-image alive by compromising our consecration. There is no truth in them.

To build our sense of dignity on the foundation of any self-images is to establish an extremely shaky structure for ourselves. We need to remember that our self-images are nothing more than the particular activities of cell systems. Cell systems are always addicted to a variety of things; their validity is never perfect, and often they are completely distorted. Thus how we view ourselves at any given time may have very little to do with how we really are. There is no way we can make an image of our true nature. In the true image of God, we ourselves are incomprehensible.

Earlier, I said that spiritual growth is movement toward increasing fulfillment of the two great commandments—deepening love for God, others, and self. Dignity is the way God begins the process of spiritual growth in us. Dignity always says we are worth far more than we can ever give ourselves credit for, that we are meant for greater things than those we ever could aspire to, and that we are more loved and more in need of love than we can ever know. Choosing dignity, then, is not selecting another self-image. It is choosing an open-endedness in which we know all our images will be insufficient. Choosing dignity is choosing spaciousness. It is an act of faith.

From a practical standpoint, choosing dignity means being vigilant about how we respond to failure in the course of our homeward journey. What happens when our addictions get the best of us, when our resolutions fail, when we see how inadequate we are, when we forget how to pray, when we lose sight of the entire process? Each of these encounters will be an opportunity for further mind tricks based on self-image. If we do not notice the tricks, we will indulge them. But if we catch the tricks early, we can simply say no. We can pick ourselves up from whatever fall we have taken and go on.

As I have said so many times before, we cannot do this alone. Left by ourselves, we simply do not have the strength either to be honest with ourselves or to claim our dignity. We must have help. Whether we like it or not, a large part of that help must come through other people.

Community

Much as we might want to avoid the humiliation of involving other people in our struggles with attachment, it becomes imperative to do so. We cannot trust our own judgments and perceptions where addiction is concerned; the mind tricks are too great. It only makes sense to recruit some independent and unbiased help.

The exact form of help will be determined in part by the nature of our attachments. Major destructive addictions demand assistance from professionals. More interior idolatries require spiritual companionship and accountability. Sometimes we just need a friend to help keep us honest. The act of seeking help might be very dramatic, as in turning oneself in to the police to put an end to repeated illegal activities. It might be joining AA or Overeaters Anonymous. It might be talking one's situation over with a pastor, counselor, or spiritual director. It might be asking one's spouse or family to help monitor a particular behavior. Whatever the form, involvement of other people is an essential component of a consecrated life. There is no authentic way around it.[5]

It is not easy to bring others into one's struggle with attachment. The thing that makes it most difficult is the very thing that makes it most helpful: it destroys the interior secrecy upon which our mind tricks thrive. Attachment makes us fool ourselves, and it makes us feel like fools in the eyes of others. Yet others' eyes are essential, for our own eyes see only what they want. We might wish it were easier, but being seen by others is part of the desert experience. There would have been no desert fathers or mothers if pilgrims had no need for companionship and guidance. The journey we take, if it is to be authentic, cannot be a private thing between ourselves and God; God is as much in our companion pilgrims as in our own souls.

We are called not only to love God above all else, but to love our companions as our very selves. Regardless of how distasteful it may be, part of this love must involve letting them see us as we are and allowing God to love us through them.

But God's grace through community involves something far greater than other people's support and perspective. The power of grace is nowhere as brilliant nor as mystical as in communities of faith. Its power includes not just love that comes from people and through people, but love that pours forth *among* people, as if through the very spaces between one person and the next. Just to be in such an atmosphere is to be bathed in healing power.

Loving power does not just happen in any random gathering. Power exists in all groups of people, but that power may or may not be gracious. Mobs have power. Armies have power. Political groups have power. Churches have power. Families have power. Like individuals, these and all other groups have addictions. They have mixed motivations. They become codependent together. They are subject to mind tricks, pride, and willfulness. They will often think they can handle it, and their attempts to do so can be far more destructive than those of individuals.

But like individuals, groups can become consecrated. With grace, they can become dedicated to their shared heart's desire for God, committed to the holy spaciousness through which grace shines most brilliantly. They can admit their collective temptation to fill the space with some object of attachment, to make an idol of a cause or of a charismatic leader or of a frozen image of God. When the members of a group consecrate themselves to God above these and all other idolatries, even above the idolatry of their own togetherness, they become a community of faith. Consecration does not make the community perfect, any more than our own consecrations make us perfect as individuals. But it claims the community's desire for perfection and, more important, its willingness to be transformed.

One of the powers of the faith community is its capacity to provide a lasting steadiness through all the waverings of its individual members. When I cannot pray, the prayer of count-less others goes on. Where I am complacent, others are strug-gling. Where I am in conflict, others are at peace. Most important, when I cannot act in loving ways, there are those in my communities who can.

For some, an even greater power comes through sacramental rites of the faith community. Sacraments such as baptism and communion represent a corporate acknowledgment and reaffir-mation of the community's consecration. They are also nodal points in the life of that community through which the power of grace may flow with unique splendor. Many people, includ-ing myself, have histories of conflict with religious institutions that make such participation difficult at times. For others, par-ticipation in sacraments has become so routine that it may seem to have lost its meaning. But these attitudes are secondary. Re-gardless of how we feel about sacraments, there can be power in them, power that is good.

Life with and in faith communities is difficult. But our strug-gles with attachment are always more difficult, and we only compound our difficulties if we deny ourselves these unique openings for grace.

Responsibility

We are part of larger systems whether we want to be or not, and if our journey is consecrated we must recognize our re-sponsibility for participating in the lovingness of those systems. At its simplest level, responsibility means respecting ourselves and those around us. In the nature of systems, all our addictive behaviors affect other people. Some behaviors really hurt oth-ers. We have a responsibility to try to identify and restrain those behaviors. In practical terms, we must listen to what other peo-ple are telling us, notice what effects we are having on them, and be willing to try to change.

Responsibility requires taking action: we need to seek grace, reach out for it, and act in accord with it. If we respond au-

thentically to God's love, we will seek nothing less than fulfillment of the great commandments. We will do all that is in our
power to love God with all our strength. We will act with kind-
ness towards others, seeking the image of God that lives within
them. And we will be as gentle and compassionate with ourselves as we possibly can. We will try to forgive others, and we
will try to forgive ourselves.

Responsibility is the real living out of consecration. Our
hearts have said yes to God, our minds have claimed the assent,
and now our actions must reflect consecration to the best of our
ability. So we live prayerfully, attempting to turn to God at all
times for guidance and being willing at all times to follow that
guidance as completely as we possibly can. Here, finally, is the
proper place of willpower in the spiritual life. We bring our
intention, our effort, our strength, and all else that we can mus-
ter to the cause of love.

We cannot, of course, be "successful." We will most certainly
fail where we try to do it autonomously. There is no way to
engineer our own salvation, to get ourselves into God's power,
because we are already there. We cannot fashion love with our
own hands, because it has already been given. In a consecrated
life, autonomous responsibility becomes a contradiction in
terms. But neither can we sit on our hands, waiting with absolute passivity for God to work miracles upon us. Passive responsibility is also a contradiction in terms.

We are neither gods nor puppets. Nor do we exist at some
point on a line between these extremes. Instead, we exist in a
dimension that is different from all such images. God is in us,
we are in God, we are in one another, and we are very much
ourselves. We are mysterious and so, therefore, is our responsibility.

For me, living with mystery means that discernment must
begin in holy spaciousness, with unknowing, and with an attitude of abject willingness. I do not, of course, mean that I do
this all the time. More often than not, I forget. But when I have
my wits about me, I try to bring all my images of self, God,

and world into God's spaciousness first, and there allow them to be opened and transfigured in whatever ways God might desire. Then, with whatever sense of guidance I have been given, and whatever insights I have gained, I try to do my best. As I go about living, I try not to leave the spaciousness behind. God is always present to me; I try, as I can, to be always present to God.

Often I do not sense any clear guidance from God, no matter how carefully I try to open myself to it. And even when I do sense it, I can never be certain that I am not deluding myself. Because of my attachments, I can be sure none of my conclusions will be perfectly pure. Yet, in the very act of sincerely seeking God's guidance, in the simple and sometimes pitiful attempts I make to turn to God, I do know that God responds. In addition, I have a head on my shoulders; I know, to some extent, what kinds of actions are loving and what are not. Further, I have Scripture and faith tradition and community to help me in the process of discernment. Once again, we are called to faithfulness, not success. We can do only what we can do.[6]

Doing what we can do means having the courage to act in accord with our best judgments, even though we know those judgments are not perfect. If we refused to act until we were completely sure of God's will, we would be committing ourselves to one or another disaster. We would either avoid responsibility by doing nothing at all or abuse responsibility by convincing ourselves that we know God's will. Authentic responsibility means acting with our best prayerful judgment, acting without complete sureness, acting in faith, but acting.

Action can be very difficult in any aspect of life, but with our major attachments it can be abysmal. The mind tricks of addiction make it excruciatingly difficult to come to any clarity about how to act. Then, when we are brought to our knees and clarity of responsible action does come, it is even more awful. It is just too simple, and we have seen it too many times before. It sits before our eyes like an ugly billboard proclaiming the two most offensive words we know: QUIT IT.

Simplicity

When it comes to dealing with addictive behavior, we might hope the final answer would be more complicated. After all, we are in the last pages of an entire book about addiction; there must be something more than those two words. No, in the context of what we can do to break addiction, all the other words simply prove that there is nothing else. It all comes down to quitting it, not engaging in the next addictive behavior, not indulging in the next temptation.

If a person is addicted to powerful chemicals that have dangerous potentials for backlash, medically supervised tapering is required. Decreasing use may prolong the quitting process for a few days or weeks, but it is still just quitting.[7]

No matter how we might want to amplify and elaborate it, stopping addictive behavior boils down to this: don't do it, refuse to do it, and keep refusing to do it. It is so simple, and it seems so impossible. Yet it was very possible for the three people whose stories I told in the last chapter. They had no fancy techniques for overcoming addiction. They had no intricate substitutions; for them there was no substitution at all. Neither did they have any complicated psychological or theological understanding to help them in their struggle. They had tried all these things before, to no avail.[8]

When these people were empowered to overcome their addictions, they did so with simplicity. They simply did not entertain the next temptation. They saw that temptation coming but neither fought it off nor turned away from it toward something else. Simply, briefly, they chose not to hop on board with it. What did they do instead? Nothing. They let their spaciousness be.

This fundamental simplicity is a consistent sign among people who have overcome addictions. It is also a sign of authentic spiritual growth. Years ago, while doing research for another book, I came across a quotation from Jan Hus, a fourteenth-century religious reformer in Czechoslovakia. As Hus was being burned at the stake for heresy, his last words were, "Oh blessed simplicity." I mentioned this during a conversation with a recovering alcoholic. He immediately pulled a card out of his wallet and handed it to me. On the card were the letters *K.I.S.S.* "This is something I got from AA," he said. "It means Keep It Simple, Stupid."

In addiction, as in all of life, we overcomplicate things in order to avoid facing their truth. The systems of our brains are intelligent, and they love to go crazy with their intellectual abilities. We can use our time thinking about the intricacies of our addictions instead of quitting them. We can fill all the potential spaces God gives us with thoughts. We can think about praying instead of praying. This does not mean we should stifle our intellects, but when we find our minds trying to pick their way through Gordian knots of thought, it would be wise to take a breath and see if we might just be avoiding some simple truth— the simple next thing we need to do, or the next temptation we should simply avoid. Ideally, the quality of simplicity will undergird and flow through all that we do. The simplicity of addiction is not to do the next addictive behavior. The simplicity of the spiritual life is living with love.

Loving Our Longing

And that, I am afraid, is about it. You may have noticed that I did not include surrender as part of a consecrated struggle with addiction. This is because we cannot do our own surrenders. To try to turn it over to God prematurely would only be another mind trick, a way of trying to escape responsibility, testing rather than trusting. But indeed God is in it with us all along, and wherever our choices are enabled to remain simple and our intent remains solid, empowerment comes through grace. There is little else we can do except to keep on trying, and looking for God's invitations and seeking simplicity.

One attitude, however, can make a fundamental difference in how we approach our attachments and our lives. It can prepare us for an embrace with God. I have alluded to it before as I have stressed the importance of claiming our longing for God, of consecrating our desire, and of being willing to tolerate spaciousness. To state it directly, we must come to love our longing.

Any authentic struggle with attachment must involve deprivation. We have to go hungry and unsatisfied; we have to ache for something. It hurts. Withdrawal symptoms are real, and, one way or another, they will be experienced. If we can both accept and *expect* this pain, we will be much better prepared to face struggles with specific attachments. We might even come to see it as birth pain, heralding the process of our delivery from slavery to freedom. If we expect comfort or anesthesia, however, we will feel more distressed when the pain of deprivation comes; we will feel like something is wrong. We will become confused and far more vulnerable to self-deception.

The implications of accepting pain are significant in dealing with specific addictions, but they become massive in terms of our basic attitude toward life. In our society, we have come to believe that discomfort always means something is wrong. We are conditioned to believe that feelings of distress, pain, deprivation, yearning, and longing mean something is wrong with the way we are living our lives. Conversely, we are convinced that a rightly lived life must give us serenity, completion, and fulfillment. Comfort means "right" and distress means "wrong." The influence of such convictions is stifling to the human spirit. Individually and collectively, we must somehow recover the truth. The truth is, we were never meant to be completely satisfied.

If God indeed creates us in love, of love, and for love, then we are meant for a life of joy and freedom, not endless suffering and pain. But if God also creates us with an inborn longing for God, then human life is also meant to contain yearning, incompleteness, and lack of fulfillment. To live as a child of God is to live with love and hope and growth, but it is also to live with longing, with aching for a fullness of love that is never quite within our grasp. As attachments lighten and idols fall, we will enjoy increasing freedom. But at the same time our hearts will feel an even greater, purer, deeper ache. This particular pain is one that never leaves us.

Authentic spiritual wholeness, by its very nature, is open-ended. It is always in the process of becoming, always incomplete. Thus we ourselves must also be always incomplete. If it were otherwise, we could never exercise our God-given right to participate in ongoing creation. The course of our lives is precisely as Saint Augustine indicated: our hearts will never rest, nor are they *meant* to rest, until they rest in God. This precious restlessness is mediated by and manifested through our physical being, through the combined minute strugglings of the cells of our brains and bodies as they seek harmony and balance in their endless adjustment to circumstances.

Our fundamental dis-ease, then, is at once a precise neurological phenomenon and a most precious gift from God. It is not a sign of something wrong, but of something more profoundly right than we could ever dream of. It is no problem to be solved, no pathology to be treated, no disease to be cured. It is our true treasure, the most precious thing we have. It is God's song of love in our soul.

Moreover, it is not simply a song sung to us from a faraway God in heaven; it is simultaneously the expression of Christ-with-and-Spirit-in us, sharing our suffering and restlessness, creating and empowering and living in and through the very cells that make us up, preserving our freedom with endless intimate love in everything we do and are. And, always, leaving us unsatisfied, calling. To claim our rightful place in destiny, we must not only accept and claim the sweetly painful incompleteness within ourselves, but also affirm it with all our hearts. Somehow we must come to fall in love with it.

I have quoted Paul on this before, but let us listen once again:

The Holy Spirit and our spirit together bear witness that we are children of God. And if we are children we are heirs as well: heirs of God and coheirs with Christ, sharing his sufferings so as to share his glory.

What we experience in this life can never be compared to the unrevealed splendor that is waiting for us. The whole creation, which was made unfulfilled by God, is waiting with eager longing, hoping to be freed. From the beginning till now all creation has been groaning in one great act of giving birth; and we too, who possess the firstfruits of the Spirit, groan inwardly as we wait to be set free.[9]

The specific struggles we undergo with our addictions are reflections of a blessed pain. To be deprived of a simple object of attachment is to taste the deep, holy deprivation of our souls. To struggle to transcend any idol is to touch the sacred hunger God has given us. In such a light, what we have called asceticism is no longer a way of dealing with attachment, but an act of love. It is a willing, wanting, aching venture into the desert of our nature, loving the emptiness of that desert because of the sure knowledge that God's rain will fall and the certainty that we are both heirs and cocreators of the wonder that is now and of the Eden that is yet to be.

Notes

Chapter 1—Desire: Addiction and Human Freedom

Epigraph: Matthew 6:21.

1. For an excellent concise synopsis of this contemporary theology, see B. McDermott, *What Are They Saying About the Grace of Christ?* (New York: Paulist, 1984). The quotation of the commandments is taken from Mark 12:29–30, which, in turn, is taken from Deuteronomy.
2. Romans 7:14–24 passim.
3. Gabriel Moran, *Religious Education Development* (Oak Grove, MN: Winston, 1983), pp. 129–56. Moran's three stages of religious development are succinct, sensible, and refreshingly simple. They begin with the stage of being "simply religious."
4. I have discussed the theme of willfulness at length in *Will and Spirit* (San Francisco: Harper & Row, 1982).
5. Genesis, chapters 1–3 passim.
6. This may not be quite accurate. To quote one translation: "When God laughs at the soul and the soul laughs back at God, the persons of the Trinity are begotten. To speak in hyperbole, when the father laughs to the son, and the son laughs back to the father, that laughter gives pleasure, that pleasure gives joy, that joy gives love, and love gives the persons [*of the Trinity*] of which the Holy Spirit is one." R. Blakney, *Meister Eckhart: A Modern Translation* (New York: Harper Torch Books, 1941), p. 245.
7. Isaiah 43:4 and 54:7–10, and 1 John 4:7–21.
8. 1 John 4:19; John 8:32–36; 15:16–17; 17:21–26; and Acts 17:25–27.
9. Adrian van Kaam, "Addiction: Counterfeit of Religious Presence," in *Personality Fulfillment in the Spiritual Life* (Wilkes-Barre, PA: Dimension Books, 1966), pp. 123–53.
10. This way of life is a system of conduct and practice known as the "Noble Eightfold Path." It is usually recorded as containing the elements of correct or "right" belief, aspiration, speech, conduct, livelihood, endeavor, mindfulness, and meditation. References for quotations in the preceding paragraph are: from the Katha Upanishad, in *The Upanishads*, trans. J. Mascaro (Baltimore: Penguin, 1965), pp. 57 and 66; Heraclitus (540–480 B.C.), quoted in D. Runes, ed., *Treasury of Philosophy* (New York: Philosophical Library, 1955), p. 501; Ecclesiastes 2:10–11.
11. Gordon S. Wakefield, ed. *The Westminster Dictionary of Christian Spirituality* (Philadelphia: Westminster, 1983), p. 111.
12. E. Colledge and B. McGinn, trans., *Meister Eckhart* (New York: Paulist, 1981), p. 294.
13. Jesus' call to love one's enemies is a demanding example of the need for detachment. His other words about detachment and love are plentiful. They

include the two great commandments; the importance of where one's treasure and heart are; giving up possessions, family, and other allegiances to follow the gospel path; the blessedness of those who are poor, who mourn, and so on. Jesus' most powerful portrayal of love as the goal of human life, however, is to be found in John's Gospel, chapter 13ff., and especially in Jesus' priestly prayer in chapter 17.

14. Metta Sutra quotation from F. Happhold, *Mysticism* (Baltimore: Penguin, 1963), pp. 171–72; Taoism quotation from Lao-tzu, *Tao Te Ching*, trans. G. Feng and J. English (New York: Random House, 1972), vii and xiii; Bhagavad Gita from J. Mascaro, trans., *The Bhagavad Gita* (Baltimore: Penguin, 1962), p. 95.

15. In Arabic, "La Illaha Illa 'lla.'" This begins the *tawhid*, the central creed of Islam.

16. Salabanda's song of realization is from "Vajra Songs: The Heart Realizations of the Eighty-four Mahāsiddhas," in *Masters of Mahamudra*, ed. K. Dowman (Albany, NY: State University of New York Press, 1985), p. 116. See also pp. 292 and 301. Bhagavad Gita quote from *Bhagavad-Gita*, trans. S. Prabhavananda and C. Isherwood (New York: New American Library, 1972), p. 129; Gandhi quotation from L. Fischer, *The Life of Mahatma Gandhi* (New York: Collier, 1950), p. 42. Note Gandhi's inclusion of devotion as preliminary to grace; Christian theology would not portray such a cause-effect relationship between devotion and grace.

17. John 3:8.

18. John of the Cross, *The Ascent of Mount Carmel*, trans. E. Peers (Garden City, NY: Image Books, 1958), p. 110.

19. Gandhi used the terms *soul force, love force,* and *force of righteousness* as translations of his doctrine of *satyagraha*. He did this to denote the necessity for personal suffering in gaining freedom from oppression. King's words (masculine language changed) are taken from his Nobel Peace Prize acceptance speech of December 1964. In the same theme he went on to say, "I believe that unarmed love and unconditional love will have the final word in reality." The holocaust quotation is from John C. Merkle, "Poetry of the Innocent from the Chambers of Hell," *Desert Call* 22, no. 1 (Spring 1987), p. 12. *Desert Call* may be obtained from the Spiritual Life Institute of America, Box 119, Crestone, CO 81131.

20. 2 Corinthians 12:7–10 (with alternative interpretation of *skolops*, stake or thorn "in the flesh"). Although there are various theories, it is not known what Paul's original context and meaning for this entire passage may have been. The words, however, speak superbly to the problem of addiction.

21. B. Ward, *The Desert Christian* (New York: Macmillan, 1980), pp. 2 and 64.

22. Luke 21:34–36.

23. Romans 5:5.

Chapter 2—Experience: The Qualities of Addiction

Epigraph: *Nicomachean Ethics*, bk. II. chap. 7.

1. Nowadays new nose drop chemicals have been invented that do not have such a dramatic rebound effect. But the labels still read, "Do not exceed

recommended dosage," and rightly so. For, as always, the new drugs have still other side effects that in some cases can be even more hazardous. From these comments, and from Sally's story in general, one could get the impression that I am against using any artificial chemicals. That is certainly not the case. Although all external drugs do disrupt internal balances, this is often necessary and sometimes life saving. My interest here is simply in describing the reactions of the body to these disturbances in the balance of opposing chemicals.

2. Matthew 5:48. What many know as "Be perfect. . . ." is rendered, in the Jerusalem Bible, as "You must set no bounds to your love. . ." See also McDermott, *What Are They Saying About the Grace of Christ?* chapter 2.

3. This theme is so integral to Jesus' message that references are too numerous to detail. I give here only a few of those from the Gospel according to Matthew: 6:19 and 25–34; 7:7; 10:37–39; 19:16–30.

4. In our culture, men and women have tended to fill different needs through their relationships. Men tend to seek affirmation of their lovability and competence, while women tend to seek affirmation of their basic human value. Although this situation is hopefully changing for the better, it still continues to the degree that men tend to be more threatened by loss of their power attachments, while women tend to be most vulnerable to their relationship attachments.

5. "Do not be afraid, for I have redeemed you; I have called you by name and you are mine. Should you pass through the sea, I will be with you . . . for you are precious in my eyes, and honored, and I love you." Isaiah 43:2–4.

6. The term *allergies* here is not only intended in the informal sense of "I'm allergic to that kind of person." The dynamics of attachment also apply to the development of physical allergies. The body's immune system, which has exceedingly close ties to brain function, operates precisely upon the same principles I will be describing in the development of addiction.

7. Romans 8:22–25.

8. Paul prefaces the above words with: "It was not for any fault on the part of creation that it was made unable to attain its purpose, it was made so by God; but creation still retains the hope of being freed, like us, from its slavery to decadence, to enjoy the same freedom and glory as the children of God." Romans 8:20–22.

Chapter 3—Mind: The Psychological Nature of Addiction

Epigraph: In *Mental Functioning*, vol. 4 of the *Collected Papers of Sigmund Freud*, trans. J. Riviere (New York: Basic Books, 1959), p. 16.

1. Luke 18:12–14.

2. A well-written and solid review of current psychiatric understandings of alcoholism and personality can be found in T. M. Donovan, "An Etiologic Model of Alcoholism," *American Journal of Psychiatry* 143, no. 1 (January 1986), pp. 1–11.

3. In fact, there are two basic forms of learning: associative and nonassociative. Associative learning requires that an association be made between a stimulus and a response, or between two stimuli. Nonassociative learning

does not require this and is therefore a simpler way of learning. There are several types of nonassociative learning. The first is *habituation,* in which one simply gets used to an unimportant stimulus that is repetitive; one responds less and less to it. The second kind of nonassociative learning is *sensitization* (sometimes called *pseudoconditioning*); after a very unpleasant experience, one tends to be more responsive to what comes next. Actually, this is not so much a learning as a simple increase in sensitivity that enhances responsiveness. *Sensory learning* also can take place without association; this involves a simple laying down of a record of sensations and is especially important in memory. *Imitative learning* is another kind of nonassociative learning in which one simply mimics what another does; this is important in language development.

In terms of associative learning, two forms are best understood. The first is *classical conditioning,* in which a "conditioned stimulus" that normally causes no response (such as a colored light) is paired with an "unconditioned stimulus" that always causes a response (such as pain). Over time, the brain associates these two stimuli, so that one learns to flinch in response to the colored light. The second form of associative learning is *operant conditioning* (also known as *trial-and-error learning*) in which a spontaneous, random behavior becomes associated with a certain stimulus. This is how rats learn a maze and how humans learn not to put their hands on hot stoves.

4. It should be noted that the feelings of pleasure or relief from pain need not really be *caused by* the behavior. They only need to occur *at the immediate time* of the behavior for the brain to make the association.

5. Conditioning is also involved in many other learning processes. If I am learning my multiplication tables, my brain is associating different sets of numbers; repetition of these associations helps to reinforce them. My learning will go faster if I experience pleasure at getting the right answers, and faster still if I have a teacher who will reward my success. If neither I nor my teacher care much about my learning, the reinforcement will be less and the learning slower. If I hate both the subject and the teacher, I am likely to be a very slow learner indeed.

6. Partial reinforcement presumably exerts its effect in a couple of ways. Most obviously, the brain learns that even after a long period of absence of reward, the possibility of good feelings remains. Thus the behavior becomes associated with additional feelings of excitement and anticipation: "Will this be the time?" "Maybe this one will work. . . ." In addition, the intermittence and unpredictability of partial reinforcement minimize any forces of *habituation* that might dampen the power of the association (see note 3).

7. This has been called, quaintly, the "Sauce Bearnaise Phenomenon," after psychologist Martin Seligman's account of developing this particular aversion from eating Béarnaise sauce when he had the stomach flu. Quoted in E. Kandel and J. Schwartz, eds., *Principles of Neural Science* (New York: Elsevier Science Publishing, 1985), p. 417. It is also one of the reasons for using the drug disulfiram in the treatment of alcoholism. Alcohol, in the presence of disulfiram, produces large amounts of toxic acetaldehyde in the body, causing serious discomfort and, possibly, aversive conditioning to alcohol.

8. F. H. C. Crick is best known for his proposal, with James Watson, of the double-helix structure of the DNA molecule. He is here quoted from "Thinking About the Brain," *Scientific American* 241, No. 3 (September 1979), pp. 221–22.

Chapter 4—Body: The Neurological Nature of Addiction

Epigraph: W. James, *The Varieties of Religious Experience* (New York: Modern Library, 1936), p. 194.

1. The old Hebrew term for soul was *nephesh*, and it meant the essence of a person in his or her wholeness. The Platonic and Neoplatonic divisions between matter and spirit had a massive effect on Western thinking but are now generally seen as archaic and outmoded. Ironically, the wholeness expressed by the more ancient Hebrew thought is now seen as much more relevant to our modern times.

2. In the precise theory of Tibetan Buddhism, human beings are seen as having three primary qualities: body, speech, and mind. *Body* reflects not only one's material being but also the physical environment within which one exists. *Speech* includes all the ways in which a person communicates and interacts with others, as well as the breath, which, as the central life-energy symbol, is most equivalent to the Western notion of "spirit." *Mind* is similar to the Western conception, but with greater emphasis on qualities of consciousness.

3. In fact, Restak himself seems to make this mistake with the word *psyche*. The actual Greek, of course, did have other words for such concepts (for example, *nous* for "mind" and *pneuma* for "spirit"). As I say, theology, and perhaps a little study of biblical Greek, might work wonders for such problems. For Restak's accounts see R. Restak, *The Brain* (New York: Bantam, 1984), pp. 342–51, esp pp. 348–49.

4. J. Changeux, *Neuronal Man* (New York: Pantheon, 1985), p. 169. I have not changed the word *man* here, inasmuch as it is in the title of both French and English versions of the book.

5. Lest I be accused of not practicing what I preach here, I have attempted to define my use of *spirit*, *soul*, *mind*, *consciousness*, and other such difficult terms in *Will and Spirit*, pp. 32–46.

6. The more generic terms *neuromediators* or *neuromodulators* have been proposed as preferable to *neurotransmitters* to include hormones and other chemicals that affect neuroreceptors but are not necessarily secreted by neurons at synapses.

7. Stimulation initiates or speeds up cell activity. Inhibition slows it down or suppresses it. Facilitation simply increases the efficiency of the receiving cell's activity, regardless of the speed or intensity of that activity.

8. Those who are familiar with the "reflex arc" of textbooks may think of such a reflex as involving only two or three neurons. One needs to keep in mind, however, that in any behavior as massive as a knee jerk, thousands of stretch receptors trigger corresponding thousands of neurons and muscle fibers.

9. Ancient Eastern medical traditions, such as acupuncture, are based on correcting imbalances of energy within bodily systems. In the West, homeopathic medicine and many new holistic approaches to healing are also centered in reestablishing equilibrium within and among such systems. In traditional Western medicine, the work of such people as Claude Bernard, who coined the term *internal milieu*, and of Hans Selye, who initiated our modern understanding of stress, has established a similar understanding of the central importance of balance and equilibrium in all bodily systems.

10. Selective inhibition indicates a basically inhibitory atmosphere in which action occurs through removing inhibition in selected areas. When I perform an activity, such as picking up a pencil, my brain initiates and governs this primarily by removing inhibition from the specific cells whose action is required for picking up the pencil, and continuing or increasing inhibition of cells whose activity is not needed or would interfere with picking up the pencil. The general atmosphere of inhibition within the brain also explains why people who suffer a stroke—loss of blood supply to the brain—may find that the paralyzed muscles in the affected part of their body become tense and spastic. Higher inhibiting neurons have been destroyed by the stroke, so the lower neurons fire excessively.

11. These studies are by now fairly well known in transpersonal psychological circles and are open to varied interpretations: B. Anand, G. Chhina, and B. Singh, "Some Aspects of Electroencephalographic Studies in Yogis," *Electroencephalography and Clinical Neurophysiology* 13 (1961): 452–56; and A. Kasamatsu and T. Hirai, "An Electroencephalographic Study of Zen Meditation," *Folia Psychiatria et Neurologia Japonica* 20 (1966): 315–36. More recent studies by Daniel Brown at Harvard and others seem to validate some of these earlier observations. Open, attentive kinds of meditation such as Soto Zen practice do indeed seem to lessen or even eradicate habituation in systems of cells that influence conscious attentiveness. Other kinds of meditation, however—especially those that emphasize great concentration—may have entirely different effects.

12. I have discussed this at some length in *Will and Spirit*, pp. 216–20.

13. The definitive work in this arena has been done by Eric Kandel, Vincent Castellucci, Irving Kupferman, and others at Columbia University using observations of the simple nervous system of the marine snail *Aplysia californica*. The implications of this work for our understanding of short- and long-term memory and learning may be profound. A number of articles have been published on these studies, but a general summary is to be found in chapter 62 of E. Kandel and J. Schwartz, eds., *Principles of Neural Science* (New York: Elsevier Science Publishing, 1985), pp. 816ff.

14. In his *Psychology of Religion*, quoted in James, *Varieties of Religious Experience*, p. 206. James says these words are the physiological equivalent of the theological statement "Man's extremity is God's opportunity."

15. The example I have used here of sedative addiction is an especially powerful one. Sedatives (barbiturates, alcohol, so-called minor tranquilizers, and the like) have such massive effects on so many cells in the brain that withdrawal can be an extremely dangerous process. If you had been taking only a small amount of sedative for a short period of time, the withdrawal symptoms may be transient and not too severe before they pass of their own accord.

But if you have been taking a lot for a long time, your brain cells can become so hyperactive in withdrawal that you may have generalized seizures and might even die.

16. Along with receptors for endorphins and enkephalins, the brain has natural receptors for adrenaline, which acts as a stimulant, and for a specific chemical that is shared by the benzodiazepine family of tranquilizers.

17. If you propose that tolerance does not enter the morning coffee routine, you should be aware of the reluctance with which I get up at the end of this precious time, the heavy sigh with which I begin the real day. I exhibit a mild attachment, and its tolerance and withdrawal symptoms are also mild. But they exist all the same.

18. In Figure 3–1, the psychological model of addiction, the spreading of addiction among systems corresponds to the "association with other experiences" component of habit formation.

19. I have referred to this phenomenon in chemical addiction as the "island experience." Physical removal from the usual setting of the addiction can be like traveling to an island of fantasy where one seems miraculously freed from the attachment's need. People can feel that the attachment is gone in such settings and be tragically surprised when they return to reality and find themselves still addicted. The island experience can also work the other way around, with a person becoming addicted in a temporary setting and then losing the attachment upon return to normal life. Summer vacation romances are one example of this, but the most profound instances in my own experience come from the Vietnam War. During that period I worked with some soldiers who had become severely addicted to pure heroin while on their tours of duty in Vietnam, went through withdrawal before returning home, and to my knowledge never had further problems with narcotic addiction. Conversely, I had occasion to see a few soldiers who had been addicted to street heroin in the United States and who never touched narcotics while in Vietnam but then returned to their habit upon completion of their duty there. Such cases are admittedly in the minority as compared to the numbers of people who began their addictions in Vietnam and continued to be addicted thereafter, but the existence of *any* such cases establishes the importance of environmental subattachments in the basic addictive process.

20. Isaiah 56:11; Habakkuk 2:5. I am also reminded of the *Preta*, or "hungry ghosts" of Tibetan Buddhism who are racked with desire, doomed to an incessant, continually defeated search for fulfillment (W. Y. Evans-Wentz, trans., *The Tibetan Book of the Dead* [London: Oxford, 1973], pp. 185–87).

Chapter 5—Spirit: The Theological Nature of Addiction

Epigraph: On his arrival in Cell 67 at Lubyanka prison. *The Gulag Archipelago* (New York: Harper & Row, 1974), pp. 184–85.

1. Psalm 139:13–14; Isaiah 43:2–4; Jeremiah 29:11; Deuteronomy 5:7 and 6:5; Leviticus 19:18. It is notable that *aheb*, the Hebrew word for love in these last passages, connotes freedom of choice; it is a purely voluntary self-

dedication. J. L. McKenzie, *Dictionary of the Bible* (New York: Macmillan, 1965), p. 520. Interestingly, McKenzie uses the words *voluntary attachment* in the definition of love.

2. T. Merton, *The Sign of Jonas* (New York: Harcourt Brace Jovanovich, 1953), p. 112. In the context of this particular quote, Merton was making the case that our natural longing for God, precisely because it is so natural and universal ("The devils desire to possess God"), is *not* necessarily inspired by grace. And without *super*natural inspiration of God, he maintained, our natural longing "means nothing at all and is without any value or merit whatsoever." In the light of his particular contemplative vocation and struggles, and certainly in the theological climate of his time, his words make a certain kind of sense. But I think it is mistaken to say that our natural hunger for God, which is a gift given to all of us *by* God, is meaningless and not inspired by grace. How we *respond* to that longing, however, may be another question altogether.

3. I cannot go into this debate in depth here. Rudolf Otto, William James, Abraham Maslow, Carl Jung, Sigmund Freud, and Rollo May are just a few psychologically oriented people who have expressed relevant points of view. Often the question itself becomes confusing, for people quickly become unclear whether longing for God implies desire for an actual sense of relationship or a more removed appreciation of meaning in life. But as I have said, I am convinced that all human beings have an inborn desire for actual personal relationship with God. This conviction comes from my own interior experience, my work in therapy with people from many cultures and countless walks of life, and my study of world religions. I further suspect that the dynamics of this longing can, and will at some point, be neurologically identified. But such specifics must be dealt with in another book.

4. Acts 17:24-28; "groping through shadows . . ." is from William Barclay's translation of the New Testament (London: William Collins Sons, 1968); Jeremiah 29:13-14.

5. Exodus 33:20, "You cannot look at my face and live."

6. Sr. Constance FitzGerald, O.C.D., beautifully portrays the relationship between this kind of impasse and the "dark night" described by John of the Cross in "Impasse and Dark Night," in *Living With Apocalypse,* ed. T. Edwards (San Francisco: Harper & Row, 1984), pp. 93-116.

7. Isaiah 44:20; John 15:4.

8. FitzGerald, "Impasse and Dark Night," p. 97.

9. In both *Will and Spirit* and *Care of Mind/Care of Spirit* (San Francisco: Harper & Row, 1982) I have discussed the relationships of self-image, unitive experience, and spiritual growth at considerable length. It is important to understand here, however, that simply losing oneself does not constitute a unitive experience. We can lose ourselves in all kinds of ways that are hardly unitive, like trances, concentration, drugs, and sleep.

10. *Lev* in Hebrew, *cardia* in Greek, this sense of heart had very little to do with the physical functions of the organ, which were unknown by the ancients. Heart was viewed as the center of a human being, the locus not only of emotion and desire but also of attention and will. The nature of a person's heart determined that person's character. Purity of heart, then, meant pu-

rity of the whole person. And the *lev shalem*, the "whole heart" with which we are meant to love God, implies the fullness of our entire being.

11. I have previously defined contemplation as direct perception without any personal manipulation of that perception, and equated it with the philosophical term *intuition* (*Will and Spirit*, pp. 24–26).

12. The distinction I have made here between the image making and the contemplative way might rightfully remind some readers of the classical *kataphatic* and *apophatic* styles of spiritual practice. When applied with grace, images can become symbols and even icons (symbols that act as windows into divine mystery) rather than idols that substitute for that mystery. Spiritual practices that rely heavily on such cellular representations of the divine are known as *kataphatic*. Most traditional practices are of this sort. Practices that seek more directly to face reality as it is and thus bypass as many cellular representations as possible are *apophatic* or, as I have defined it, contemplative. It is important to note that my distinctions here apply only to the practices or means of approaching spiritual experience. The nature of the experience itself seems to me to be beyond such distinctions.

13. Very briefly, *karma* is the endless universal reverberation of effects of action, causing further action. Dependent origination, *pratītya-samutpāda* in Sanskrit, is the Buddha's elaboration on *karma*. It also refers to a chain of events arising not from action but from conditions. Since Buddhism holds that there is no metaphysical reality apart from the mind that conceives it, these conditions are almost invariably assumed to be states of mind, the first of which is *avidyā*, or ignorance.

14. From the poem "Eternity" in W. Blake, *Poems and Prophecies* (New York: Dutton, 1970), p. 383.

15. Ecclesiastes 2:10–11; Psalm 119:29 and 92.

16. Jeremiah 29:11–14; Isaiah 43:2–3.

17. Matthew 6:24; 10:37; 11:29–30.

18. In *Will and Spirit* (pp. 265–72), I have given a description of Western thought concerning the origins of evil.

19. For temptation as seduction by the devil: 1 Corinthians 7:5, 1 Thessalonians 3:5, and 1 Peter 5:8ff.; as an independent force: Galatians 6:1–8 and 2 Peter 2:9; as part of the human condition: 1 Corinthians 10:13; as something to be grateful for: James 1:2.

20. James 1:13.

21. Deuteronomy 8:3–6.

22. Revelation 22:17.

Chapter 6—Grace: The Qualities of Mercy

Epigraph: Excerpts from John 1:4, 5, 14, and 16. This beautiful prologue to John's Gospel may have been taken from a popular Greek hymn of the times, and verse 16 is, in my opinion, one of the finest human attempts to find words for the indescribable abundance of God's grace. The Greek words, *Kai ek tou pleromatos auton emeis pantes elabomen, kai charin anti charitos*, might literally be "And of his fullness we all received, and grace upon grace." The final phrase pleads for an appreciation of overflowing abundance of love: "grace for grace," "full of grace and truth," or "one gift replacing another."

1. Psalms 42:1–2 and 63:1; Isaiah 35:6–7; 41:18–20; 51:3; and 58:11.

2. I again refer you to Brian McDermott's excellent review of grace: *What Are They Saying About the Grace of Christ?* There are, of course, a variety of theological distinctions concerning the qualities of grace. Perhaps the most obvious, and most crude, is between grace that appears miraculously, as "divine intervention," in the course of life, and the grace that is given inherently in our natural creation. Modern Christian theology seems to be in fairly substantial agreement that this latter, "natural" grace is not something just planted in us at our creation; it is *constantly* given to us by God.

3. Explaining the why of parental love is not the same as explaining how it happens. There is quite a bit of how information related to brain function. Paul MacLean, for example, talks of the second stage of the triune brain (that associated with mammals) as being characterized by the capacity for maternal care (Restak, *The Brain*, p. 136). In higher mammals at least, one would expect this to be associated with feelings of affection as well as caretaking behaviors. As in our discussion of suffering and attachment, to say that such feelings and behaviors exist to promote the survival of species is an insufficient why. It is only part of the how of survival. Any legitimate why must somehow be related to the Big Why: Why does this creation exist in the first place? Why is there anyone to survive or anything to survive for? And this, of course, returns us promptly to God's grace.

4. Isaiah 57:16.

5. Elizabeth of the Trinity, a French Carmelite, was well known at the turn of the century for her prayer, which began with a hymn to the changelessness of God's love: "Oh my God, Trinity whom I adore, help me to forget myself entirely that I may be established in You as still and as peaceful as if my soul were already in eternity. May nothing trouble my peace or make me leave You, O my Unchanging One, but may each minute carry me further into the depths of Your Mystery." *Elizabeth of the Trinity: The Complete Works*, trans. A. Kane (Washington, DC: Institute for Carmelite Studies, 1984), vol. 1, p. 183.

6. The "practice of the presence" of God is an attempt to decrease habituation and to enable a moment-by-moment attentiveness to God throughout the day. In Christianity, this practice is connected to the admonitions of Jesus and Paul to "pray constantly." In Hinduism, a similar practice is called "witnessing," and in Buddhism, "mindfulness."

7. I am saying, in effect, that there are dimensions of the human spirit, however small, that remain forever free from determination by the brain. Such a statement goes right to the heart of brain/mind or brain/spirit debate, which has existed for generations: are all our choices absolutely predestined by our organic genetic makeup and subsequent conditioning, or are there points and places where will or spirit is truly free? I hope in future works to be able to develop my thoughts and reasons more explicitly in this arena, but to try to do so here would require far more details and theoretical models than space permits. I can say, however, that at the time of this writing there is no hard physical data to prove or even substantively support *either* side of the debate.

8. Mark 9:24.
9. May, *Will and Spirit*, pp. 25 and 53.
10. Matthew 21:24.
11. Exodus 1–15.
12. Isaiah 51:3.
13. We often associate repentance with guilt, pain, shame, and the like, from its Latin root *poena*, pain. Although repentance surely includes a painful acknowledgment of guilt, it more basically refers to a "change of heart." The Greek word *metanoia* reflects this. And it may help to know that the biblical Hebrew word for repentance was *nacham*, "to be comforted" or "eased."
14. Luke 4:1–13; Matthew 4:1–11; Mark 1:12–13. The account of Jesus' forty days in the wilderness is an intentional reprise of Israel's forty years in the desert, in which Jesus is presented as the new Moses.

Chapter 7—Empowerment: Grace and Will in Overcoming Addiction

Epigraph: Mark 10:26–27.

1. The desert fathers and mothers sought a state called *apatheia*, the absence of attachment, and they carefully distinguished it from *accidia*, a dull, lethargic absence of caring and interest. Our modern understanding of the word *apathy* is unfortunate here, for while *apatheia* was the psychological goal of the desert monks, *accidia*, which is true apathy, was their worst psychological enemy. They called it "the demon of the noonday sun," and they understood clearly how it could plague anyone who was seeking freedom from attachment. Religious history is replete with stories of extreme renunciations and self-mortifications in the name of asceticism. Though such dramatic struggles with attachment stand out in one's memory, the reality of spiritual searching has generally been much more moderate. Anthony the Great, one of the foremost desert monks of early Christianity, said, "Renounce this life . . . despise the flesh, so that you may preserve your souls." But he also said, "If we push ourselves beyond measure we will break; it is right for us from time to time to relax our efforts." *The Desert Christian*, trans. B. Ward (New York: Macmillan, 1975), pp. 8 and xxi.
2. Matthew 11:18–19. The actual words are "Now the Son of Man comes . . ." *Son of Man* is a specific messianic title Jesus chose for himself from Daniel and Enoch.
3. Matthew 23:24; 6:1–6; 15:11.
4. The fear that freedom will remove creativity and richness from life is also commonly encountered in relation to psychotherapy. Thinking about depth psychotherapy, people frequently say something like, "All the greatest artists and writers, and all the other really creative people of history, were neurotic in one way or another. And the most well adjusted people I know seem rather boring. I would never want to become so well adjusted as to lose my creativity." This kind of concern has been so common that studies have been done to test it. Results show there is no basis in fact whatsoever

for it. What lies behind the concern is simply the normal human fear of change. We become so dependent upon our sense of who we are that we fear becoming anything more. In words from Hamlet, it makes us "rather bear those ills we have than fly to others that we know not of" (act III, scene 1).

5. In the course of my work, I have been privileged to meet a large number of authentically recognized holy people from a variety of religious traditions: monks and hermits, gurus and swamis, lamas and Zen masters. I have also encountered some of the simple holy people we all meet from time to time; known only to their families and friends, and never claiming holiness, they are transparent windows of God's grace. My life has been deeply enriched by meeting these people; I have always been inspired and enabled by them. They have mediated grace for me in sometimes quite spectacular ways. But they all have their egos, they all have their problems, and they all have addictions. They are certainly *less* attached than you or I might be, and most are more aware of the addictions they do have, but they are human; none is completely free. And, I must add, though God seems to work through such people in very special ways and I recall my encounters with them vividly, the people who have most mediated grace for me have been the regular, ordinary persons with whom I have happened to live my life.

6. In this list of examples, I have not included the clinical substitution of methadone for heroin as part of the treatment of narcotic addiction. Although this is a real substitution of one addictive drug for another, the primary effect is not to change the basic addiction but simply to substitute a legal drug for an illegal one. The step can be a constructive one, because it may help addicts modify associated behaviors (multisystem involvements) such as hustling, buying, dealing, stealing, and the like. The hope is that addicts will thereby be sufficiently freed from their associated activities to concentrate on dealing with the primary addiction. Sometimes this does happen. More commonly, however, the benefits of methadone maintenance programs have been like those of legalized heroin programs in other countries: they affect the larger social systems by decreasing criminal behavior.

7. John of the Cross described this transformative process in terms of passing through the nights of sense and soul. He also used the image of ascending Mount Carmel. Teresa of Avila described it in images of moving through the mansions of the "interior castle." A number of translations of their works are available; the Institute for Carmelite Studies in Washington, D.C., is the best resource.

8. When it occurs in the midst of mind tricks, the notion of surrendering to God as a way of overcoming addiction can be dangerous. It can lead to faked surrenders, false rock bottoms. By definition, rock bottom can come only with *purgation*, the complete exhaustion of self-serving manipulations. When it is faked, it not only perpetuates the addiction; it can also establish the foundation for even more serious distortions of spiritual surrender. I have discussed some of the dangers of distorted and misplaced surrenders in *Will and Spirit*, pp. 299–309.

9. Again I must acknowledge the theological imprecision of my descriptions of the manifestations of grace. I hope to develop some of this in future

works. By *supernatural* here, I am simply returning to that crude distinction between the grace that God continually gives us through our nature (natural) and that which is given in special, more evidently miraculous, ways (supernatural). Suffice it to say that all grace is miraculous, and yet all, in God's terms, is very natural. If you wish to look into this further, I once again refer you to Brian McDermott, *What Are They Saying About the Grace of Christ?*

10. I have no hard evidence as to what actually happens to cellular systems in such deliverances. My impression, based simply on the consequent behavior of people, is that the most common change is a lessening of multisystem involvements. It is as if many of the systems associated with the addiction are enabled to relax, and the person winds up with a much *simpler* approach to the addictive behavior. But the empowering does not take the form of an ability to fight off addictive behavior forcibly. It is something more gentle than that.

11. Matthew 12:43–45; Luke 11:24–26. Many biblical accounts of healings and exorcisms bear out the notion that deliverance happens as part of a process that is meant to be ongoing. Repeatedly, Jesus affirms that "your faith has made you whole," indicating a preexisting condition of willingness on the part of the one who is healed. He adds a strong imperative to act upon what has happened, a continuing invitation in which the one who is healed is meant to participate. Jesus instructs the healed one to go forth with some special intent, made possible by the healing.

12. The roots of the word *salvation* seem to me of special significance here. In Latin, Greek, and Hebrew, salvation immediately refers to safety. Behind this, in the Hebrew root *YS,* is the connotation of space and freedom. Safety, then, comes with space within which one is free. Biblically, this is contrasted with the Hebrew root *SRR:* narrowness, constraint. J. McKenzie, *Dictionary of the Bible* (New York: Macmillan, 1965), p. 760.

13. Brother Lawrence, *The Practice of the Presence of God,* trans. Sr. Mary David (New York: Paulist, 1978), p. 89.

Chapter 8—Homecoming: Discernment and the Consecrated Life

Epigraph: Romans 8:14–39 passim.

1. Many resources exist for those who wish to pursue the subject of spiritual discernment. I have discussed it in *Will and Spirit,* pp. 287–93, and at even greater length in *Care of Mind/Care of Spirit* (San Francisco: Harper & Row, 1982). The most famous and now classical approach to discernment is that of Saint Ignatius Loyola. For an excellent contemporary version of this, see T. Green, *Weeds Among the Wheat* (Notre Dame, IN: Ave Maria, 1984). A good brief overview of several approaches can be found in K. Leech, *Soul Friend* (San Francisco: Harper & Row, 1977).

2. In the original Aramaic that Jesus used, the prayer was probably simpler still, something like, "Forgive us our offenses, for we also forgive our debtors, and let us not fall into temptation." See Joachim Jeremias, *The Prayers of Jesus* (Naperville, IL: Alec R. Allenson, 1967), pp. 94–95.

3. There are so many meditation books and programs available that I will not further describe the techniques here. I especially recommend T. Edwards, *Living in the Presence* (San Francisco: Harper & Row, 1987), as a contemporary manual for a variety of such practices. I do emphasize, however, that there are many different kinds of meditation, each of which has its own place and purpose. The contemplative form I am describing is but one of these. For those who study such things, it may be clarifying to say that I am describing mindfulness meditation rather than concentration meditation. In classical Christian language, I am not describing meditation *per se* but rather a seeking of contemplation.

4. Benedicta Ward, trans., *The Desert Christian* (New York: Macmillan, 1980), p. 172.

5. Many helping groups exist for the most obvious and/or destructive addictions. Examples include the "anonymous" groups for alcoholism, narcotic and other drug addiction, overeating, gambling, and neuroses; support groups and clinical programs for anorexia and bulimia; stop-smoking groups; specialized programs for phobias, shoplifting, child or spouse abuse, and sexual difficulties; stress-reduction and workaholic support groups; groups of adult children of alcoholics, and many others. One great advantage of such specialized groups is that members know the specific mind tricks associated with their particular attachment and can point them out with great efficiency as well as profound understanding. Local mental health associations can provide contacts with these groups.

6. Discernment is always open-ended, never finalized. Saint Ignatius Loyola, originator of the most precise processes of discernment, was very careful to point out that our attempts to discern God's will can be accurate only "to some extent."

7. This includes but is not limited to alcohol, barbiturates, tranquilizers and other sedatives, or amphetamines and other stimulants that have been used in substantial amounts over considerable time. Any attempt to deal with significant chemical addiction should include medical consultation, because the interplay of the abused chemicals with one's own internal chemistry is too complex to be handled safely on one's own.

8. As a reminder in terms of aversion addictions, this "don't do it, refuse to do it, and keep refusing to do it" translates in simple reverse. In the case of a phobic or prejudicial attachment, for example, it means "don't avoid it, refuse to avoid it, and keep refusing to avoid it."

9. Romans 8:16–23 passim.

Index

Meditation, 8, 44, 89, 126, 151; attentive, 166; and habituation, 76; and spiritual growth, 104, 106
Mental retardation, 162–63
Merton, Thomas, 92
Methadone, 147n.6
Midlife crisis, 95
Mind tricks, 40–52, 60, 166–68
Money. *See* Possessions
Morphine. *See* Narcotics
Motivation, 40, 53–54, 60; and neurology, 82
Multi-system involvement, 85–86

Narcotics, 5, 10, 69, 83–84, 96
Neurology, 64–90; and deliverance, 154n.10; and faith, 128; of spiritual growth, 104–6; and trust, 29
Neurons, 66–79, 87, 93; and attachment, 78–83; groups of, 67–68; systems of, 67–68, 72, 82. *See also* Neurology, Synapses
Neuroreceptors. *See* Synapses
Neurotransmitters. *See* Synapses
Newton, John, 125
Nicotine, 9, 69
Normality, 78, 80, 106, 148
Nose drops, 24–26

Obsession, 13–14, 25
Overeating, 86

Passion, 2 (*def.*), 141. *See also* Desire
Paul, Saint, 2, 20, 40, 92, 94, 162, 180
Pavlov, Ivan, 55
Penfield, Wilder, 64–66
Phobias, 36, 44, 61–62, 113
Physiology, 22–24. *See also* Neurology
Poeman, Abba, 168
Possessions, 32–33, 93
Power, 33
Prayer, 8, 44, 85, 126, 151; as addiction, 167; contemplative, 165; honesty in, 168–69; Lord's, 165n.2; and spiritual growth, 104, 106; and stress, 87–89
Prejudice, 36, 39, 113
Pride, 19, 48
Psychoanalysis, 27, 52–55
Psychosis, 50, 162
Psychotherapy, 51

Rationalization, 24–27, 43
Rebound reaction. *See* Withdrawal symptoms
Reformation of addictive behavior, 146–49
Reinforcement. *See* Conditioning
Relationship, 33, 92
Repentance, 134, 136, 137n.13 (*def.*), 165
Repression, 1–3, 43–45, 76, 107–8
Resistance, 142–46
Responsibility, 111, 121, 139; in consecration, 174–76
Restak, Richard, 64
Rock bottom, 10, 19, 48, 95

Salvation, 17, 160n.12
Satan. *See* Evil
Security, 31–36, 93
Sedatives, 27, 80–83; withdrawal, 82n.15, 177n.7
Self deception, 27–28, 35, 43–50
Self esteem, 22, 42 (*def.*), 60
Self image. *See* Self representation
Self representation, 53, 59, 83, 98–103; and dignity, 169–71
Shalem Institute, viii
Simplicity, 177–78
Sin, 2, 114
Solzhenitsyn, Aleksandr, 91
Soul, 19, 64n.1
Spaciousness, vi, 31, 147, 149, 175–76; and contemplation, 160; of self, 101, 103
Spirit: and brain, 64–66; Holy, 17, 92, 123, 137, 180; human, 18, 39, 92 (*def.*)
Spiritual experiences, 7, 98–103, 153
Spiritual growth, 53, 97, 103–9, 128, 154, 162; and dignity, 171
Spirituality: apophatic and kataphatic, 108n.12
Spiritual warfare, 89
Starbuck, Edwin, 80n.14
Stimulants, 83n.16; withdrawal, 177n.7
Stress, 26–27, 73 (*def.*), 82; addiction to, 86–89; responses to, 73–78
Struggle: stage of attachment, 59–60
Substitution of addictions, 147–49
Superstition, 138
Surrender, 48, 139